Debates in Indian Philosophy

Debates in Indian Philosophy
Classical, Colonial, and Contemporary

A. Raghuramaraju

OXFORD
UNIVERSITY PRESS

OXFORD
UNIVERSITY PRESS

YMCA Library Building, Jai Singh Road, New Delhi 110 001

Oxford University Press is a department of the University of Oxford.
It furthers the University's objective of excellence in research, scholarship,
and education by publishing worldwide in

Oxford   New York
Auckland   Cape Town   Dar es Salaam   Hong Kong   Karachi
Kuala Lumpur   Madrid   Melbourne   Mexico City   Nairobi
New Delhi   Shanghai   Taipei   Toronto

With offices in
Argentina   Austria   Brazil   Chile   Czech Republic   France   Greece
Guatemala   Hungary   Italy   Japan   Poland   Portugal   Singapore
South Korea   Switzerland   Thailand   Turkey   Ukraine   Vietnam

Oxford is a registered trade mark of Oxford University Press
in the UK and in certain other countries.

Published in India
by Oxford University Press, New Delhi

© Oxford University Press 2006

ISBN-13: 978-0-19-567151-3
ISBN-10: 0-19-567151-1

Typeset in Aldine401 BT 10/12
by Eleven Arts, Keshav Puram, Delhi 110 035
Printed in India by Rakmo Press Pvt. Ltd., New Delhi 110 020
Published by Manzar Khan, Oxford University Press
YMCA Library Building, Jai Singh Road, New Delhi 110 001

To
Professor P.R.K. Rao
Remembering the wonderful intellectual ambience at IIT Kanpur

■

Contents

■

Preface

Why are there no significant debates in contemporary Indian philosophy when debates and dialogues were the nerve centre of classical Indian philosophy? This question has not been addressed in the standard works that reflect the contemporary philosophical situation in India, and hence this volume attempts to move outside and into the contemporary political domain in search of a viable answer.

An attempt is made to highlight the points of difference for debate as available in the sphere of contemporary Indian philosophy. In this process, the work goes beyond (i) the ascendancy model proposed by Partha Chatterjee, namely, moments ascending from Bankim to Nehru through Gandhi, and (ii) the attempts, which sought to collapse the differences between, for instance, Vivekananda and Gandhi or Aurobindo and Krishnachandra Bhattacharyya. On the contrary, this work highlights the available differences, and not necessarily the postmodernist versions of difference. The postmodern version within the West is largely stuck within the prism of the 'romantic problematic', which need not be the predicament of difference in India. Difference in India can become a political programme. In highlighting the debates between different contemporary Indian philosophers, this work strives to break open the current terrain of philosophical discussions on classical Indian philosophy and contemporary Western philosophy, *a la* B.K. Matilal, J.N. Mohanty, and others. Exposing the underlying imbalance and ensuing politics is one of the implicit purposes of this work. Explicitly, my present endeavour is to elaborate the islands of difference within contemporary Indian thought, nurture them by rejuvenating debates, which set in motion the internal philosophical activity. One might indeed detect in this book the pervasive presence of the perceptions of the pre-modern non-classical India, embodied in the works of Mahatma Gandhi and Ashis Nandy.

I have, at places, reproduced long quotations, which I have chosen not to paraphrase, as some of these writings are not easily available. Further, I want the thinkers dealt within the work to speak for themselves as much as possible. This is necessitated because: one, I have serious problems with the way these thinkers are presented in certain well-known works; and, two, I strongly feel that in my work these thinkers have been presented in a new light thus necessitating extensive quotations to reinforce these points. Above all, extensive quotations can facilitate critical responses of the reader to my point of view. I have retained the spellings within quotations, such as K.C. Bhattacharya for Krishnachandra Bhattacharyya, as they are.

Here let me share a significant feature of this volume. The reader may find an obvious similarity in the line of argument and in my juxtapositions of various thinkers and scholars discussed here. But while this may look obvious after being written, this was not so when I first started working on the volume. I had no readymade material at my disposal while working on this book, and had to glean information from different sources and 'assemble' them. I also had to constantly come up with comparisons and contrasts, perhaps for the first time. I had to not only explicate the terms of the debate between major thinkers like Swami Vivekananda and Mahatma Gandhi, V.D. Savarkar and Gandhi, and Sri Aurobindo and Krishnachandra Bhattacharyya, but also bring together, perhaps for the first time, scholars like Sudhir Kakar and Tapan Raychaudhuri, to compare and contrast.

Though the ideas put forth in this book started taking shape in my mind at IIT Kanpur, they travelled with me to Goa University and grew substantially in the wonderful ambience there, helped by significant inputs from R.A. Sinari, A.V. Afonso, Sasheej Hegde, Alito Sequeria, R.V. Joshi, Y.S. Prahlad, P.M. Reddy, and many others. The department of philosophy gave me an opportunity to teach the course on contemporary Indian philosophy, which helped me focus on systematic readings in this area. I continued to teach this course when I moved to the University of Hyderabad. Except Chapter 1, which was first written while I was still in Goa, the rest of the chapters were written in Hyderabad. They were presented in seminars at the Indian Institute of Advanced

Study, Shimla, Sahitya Akademi, Centre for the Study of Developing Societies, Sri Shankaracharyya University of Sanskrit, Kalady, and the Konrad Adenauer Foundation, New Delhi. I wish to thank Mrinal Miri, U.R. Anantamurthy, K. Sachidanandan, Ashis Nandy, T.N. Madan, Madhu, Koshy Abey, and Helmut Reifield for their kind invitations. I would also like to express my gratitude to my teachers at the University of Hyderabad—Ramachandra Gandhi, Suresh Chandra, Y.N. Chopra, and S.A. Zaidi—for introducing me to philosophy.

Javeed Alam and S.G. Kulkarni gave me their detailed critical comments and suggestions for which I am thankful to them. I thank Jyotirmaya Sharma for generously helping me locate references on Savarkar. I would have perhaps finished this work many years later but for Arpita's encouragement and reminders, for which I am grateful to her. Thanks also to Venkat Rao, Hargopal, I Iaribabu, Sridhar, Alladi Uma, Bhargavi Davar, Nizar Ahmed, V. Sanil, Prajit K. Basu, Satya P. Gautam, M. Krishnaiah, K. Laxminarayana, Manjari Katzu, Aniket Alam, Anindita Mukhopadhyaya, Vasanti Srinivasan, Naresh-Shobha, I Iarnoor, and my students Minu Mohan, Gautam Satpathy, and J. Antony Juno Jesa. Parul Nayyar made important corrections for which I am grateful to her. I am also thankful to the editors at Oxford University Press and the two referees for their critical comments.

Some parts of the discussion, particularly on Savarkar and Gandhi, were earlier published in *Mahatma Gandhi and Communal Harmony*, edited by Asghar Ali Engineer and published by the Gandhi Peace Foundation in 1997. I also wish to thank the following publishers for allowing me to quote from their publications: Popular Prakashan, Mumbai; Manchester University Press, Manchester; Motilal Banarsidass Publishers Pvt. Ltd, New Delhi; Palgrave Macmillan; Bharatiya Vidya Bhavan; Indian Council of Philosophical Research, New Delhi; and Springer Science and Business Media, Berlin.

■

CHAPTER ONE

The Discourse of Debates in Indian Philosophy
Classical, Colonial, and Contemporary

Distrust agreement and find in dissent the confirmation of your own intuitions.

—Umberto Eco, *Travels in Hyperreality*, p. xii.

By insisting that the unity of the world is not a given but is constituted through dialogue and communication, I wanted to make room for the centrality of dialogue in politics. Political truth is no one's a priori gift; it emerges through conversation. What is there to begin with, is not truth but a standpoint or standpoints. There is a danger lurking in the Gandhian idea of *satyâgraha*, for it might become an obstinate clinging to one's standpoint. But clinging to truth demands ceaseless effort to arrive at the truth. In politics, there is no solipsistic way of arriving at it. Political truth has to be brought about through conversation.

—J.N. Mohanty, *The Self and Its Other: Philosophical Essays*, p. 25.

I

The widespread philosophical activity in India that prevailed before the advent of colonialism, subsequently showed substantial decline. Referring to the early philosophical activity in India, Kalidas Bhattacharyya says:

'Traditional Indian philosophy' is the corpus of philosophical doctrines and dissertations that have been current in India for at least two millenniums and communicated from generation to generation mainly through Sanskrit language and largely also through Pali...and Prakrit... The beauty of the whole tradition is that it was a perfectly living widespread study among Indian philosophers till only the other day—till, one may say, a hundred and twenty-five years back... This was the case even during the whole period of Muslim rule in India. (1982: 171–2)

This, however, has faded away, though not in entirety but in significant parts during the contemporary period. This fading was not internally necessitated, as perhaps seems to be the case between modernity and tradition within the West, but externally enforced. through colonial intervention during the last one 'hundred and twenty-five years'.[1] Without maintaining that there was either uninterrupted or uniform development of philosophical activity prior to colonialism, however, an attempt is made here to note the nature of the changing patterns of philosophical activity consequently.

Instead of merely denouncing these interventions, this book seeks to retrace through 'complex strategies' the changes the Indian mind underwent during colonialism, identify the range of interactions, and elucidate the nature and extent of the success of these interactions. Particularly, it focuses on the changing patterns of the dialogical structure of Indian thought. More specifically, it rallies around the question, 'What accounts for the decline of debates in Contemporary Indian Philosophy?' That this decline begs investigation is bolstered by the fact that debates and dialogues embodied the hub of classical Indian philosophy. This is best exemplified in the foundational texts of Indian philosophy such as the Upanishads, which contain lively dialogues between sages like Aruni, Svetaketu, Narada, Sanat Kumar, Prajapati, Yajnavalkya and significantly Gargi and Maitreyi. The philosophical heat continued to maintain itself in debates between the orthodox and heterodox schools, and even within them. In fact, it was mandatory that any system builder or sub-system builder or interpreter should consider the actual and possible objections against his or her point of view. Actually, some philosophers could put forth the opponent's point of view more ably and effectively than the opponent himself or herself. Vacaspati Misra is an illustrious example of this. Referring to the debates in classical India 'prevalent probably as early as the time of Buddha and the Mahavira (*Jina*)', B.K. Matilal says:

Logic developed in ancient India from the tradition of *vâdavidyâ*, a discipline dealing with the categories of debate over various religious, philosophical, moral, and doctrinal issues. There were several *vâda* manuals available around the beginning of the Christian era. They were meant for students who wanted to learn how to conduct debates successfully, what tricks to learn, how to find loopholes in the opponent's position, and what pitfalls to be wary of... Of these manuals, the one found in the *Nyâyasûtras* of Aksapâda Gautama (circa AD 150) is comparatively more systematic than others....

Debates, in Aksapâda's view, can be of three types: (i) an honest debate (called *vâda*) where both sides, proponent and opponent, are seeking the truth, that is, wanting to establish the right view; (ii) a tricky debate (called *jalpa*) where the goal is to win by fair means or foul; and (iii) a destructive debate (called *vitandâ*) where the goal is to defeat or demolish the opponent, no matter how... The first kind signals the employment of logical arguments, and use of rational means and proper evidence to establish a thesis. It is said that the participants in this kind of debate were the teacher and the student, or the students themselves, belonging to the same school

The second was, in fact, a winner-takes-all situation... Tricks, false moves, and unfair means were allowed according to the rules of the game....

The third type was a variety of the second type, where the winner was not supposed to establish his own position...but only to defeat the opponent using logical arguments, or as the case was, tricks or clever devices. (1999: 2–3)

Such philosophical activity with debates at its centre, widespread during classical times, has since faded away. There is a consensus regarding the agency—both internal to the tradition and external to it—causing this. For instance, pointing out the indomitable presence of Western philosophy and the severity of its impact on philosophy in India, Kalidas Bhattacharyya says:

Most of the others who have done philosophy in India since have more or less servilely accepted Western philosophy, and that too as it was understood by the British thinkers, and granted recognition to that much only of Indianism which was intelligible, in terms of Western ideas. The rest was rejected as dogmatic, magical, tribal, romantic, speculative and what not? (1982:173)

He, however, simultaneously identifies the problems and difficulties with the 'old-type' of present-day scholars of Indian philosophy. About them he says:

The difficulty with these old-type scholars in Indian philosophy is that they live in a self-contained world of their own and do not care to communicate with others except in their own limited world... This was the state of affairs even in the old-day India.[2] (1982: 173–4)

While acknowledging the fact that Western education has done India incalculable harm, he however, recognizes that it 'has after all restored to us that one world'. He warns that the continuing seclusion could only lead to 'inbreeding in the field of ideas', and this would be only 'false patriotism and harmful nostalgia'. Referring to the purview of seclusion S.N. Dasgupta says that the pandits were not only ignorant about new ideas from the outside but were equally unaware of other Indian systems. He says:

Even the best Pandits of our age follow the old traditional method, and are almost always profoundly ignorant of Buddhism and Jainism...and with few exceptions, they seldom publish anything which may be said to embody the results of their study and mature thinking. (1982: 220)

Further, pointing out yet another limitation within classical Indian philosophy in Sanskrit by pandits of the twentieth century, M.P. Rege, who made many innovative attempts to initiate dialogues between classical pundits and modern logicians, says:

Indian philosophy gives the impression of moving in a closed circle. The discussions, no doubt, are free, but *all* the *pûrva-paksas* are given. The arguments which can be advanced in their support or for defending them against possible attacks are well-known. The possible counter-arguments from the side of the *siddhânta* are also well-rehearsed... The new argument is much likely to be a variation on an old argument... They could only produce improvements in style, not in substance.[3] (Rege in his Introduction in Daya Krishna, et al. 1991: xxiii)

So we have both internal and external reasons, the former more dominant, for the decay of philosophical thinking, thus settling the question who caused the decay. This clarity, however, proves elusive regarding other questions, namely, 'Why did this change take place; is it desirable or not?' and 'What is the picture of the mind consequent to this change?'.

First, let us try and answer why the decay took place. Unlike the ambivalence of Kalidas Bhattacharyya's views, many like S.N. Dasgupta wholesomely welcomed the intervention of Western philosophy. He writes:

The torrents that are coming are not merely a passing inundation. They indicate a rise of water which has come to stay and increase. If we try to hold fast to our old bedrock and turn a deaf ear to the roaring rush we are bound to be drowned and suffocated... We would rather be washed away, or clutch at a floating rafter, and save overselves than hold fast to the old bedrock beneath the waters. Our real chance of life, therefore, is neither to hold fast to the submerged rock, nor to allow ourselves to be washed away, but to build an edifice of our own, high and secure enough to withstand the ravages of all inundations. We want to avail ourselves of all that come floating to us and enjoy them at our home. Let the waters of the Western sea come and break themselves on the walls of our fortress with their foaming billows. Our only safety is thus to be with the sea and yet above it. (1982: 215–16)

The first part of the above statement by Dasgupta,[4] though in a descriptive mode, represents a form which foresees the inevitability of the British intervention. The second part, on the other hand, reveals his desire to be above the British impact. Striking a more balanced note while elucidating different phases in contemporary Indian thought, P.T. Raju says:

The work of understanding and interpreting Western thought in terms of the Indian and of the Indian in terms of the Western became, therefore, very important; and educated Indians, who felt a responsibility to their own culture and spiritual life, thought that such a task was an absolute necessity. (1985: 539)

This turning away from the West, though not shunning it, to study Indian thought, says Raju, 'produced all the great philosophers in the last few decades in India' who are the 'products of the Indian Renaissance' and they are 'greatly influenced by the East and the West'. (1985: 541–2)

Thus, while Dasgupta believes in the inevitability, and of course, desirability of Western intervention, Bhattacharyya is critical of it and Raju emphasizes the different stages contemporary Indian thought has passed through. An important feature of these views is that they do accept in varying degrees the positive aspects of the British while still making a case for Indian thought. This introspection along with concern for their own is the dominant feature of these thinkers. While Bhattacharyya invokes a need for self-introspection in the context of defending Indian thought, Dasgupta's statement is more in the form of a warning.

Though there is a range of reactions to the 'why' question,[5] regarding the desirability or otherwise of colonial intervention, the answer to the 'what' question, regarding the nature of Indian thought subsequent to this intervention, is not sufficiently grasped. That is, while we have a range of conflicting views regarding the normativity of colonial intervention, there are not many who present an account of the 'impact' of colonialism on the Indian mind. However, it is necessary to focus on such an account, both for those who want to leave the past behind as well as those who desire to positively negotiate with the past. Unless the structure of the Indian mind following this intervention is sufficiently understood and analysed, attempts by both critics as well as advocates of these changes would be found wanting. In this context it is important to take note of yet another view, that of thinkers like Sri Aurobindo who explain away the impact of colonialism on Indian society as not very deep. Perhaps, Sri Aurobindo, like Ananda Coomaraswamy, thinks that the Indian soul came out unscathed from the colonial onslaught though its body was badly damaged. Sri Aurobindo says:

The Indian brain is still in potentiality what it was; but it is being damaged, stunted and defaced. The greatness of its innate possibilities is hidden by the greatness of its surface deterioration. ('The Brain of India', Vol. 3, 1972: 339)

In contrast, there are thinkers according to whom Indian philosophy, and thus the Indian mind, was virtually destroyed by colonial intervention. Daya Krishna, who warns us against the possibility of Indian philosophy remaining merely a subject of antiquarian interest and research, characterizes the present picture of Indian philosophy as 'dead and mummified'. (1996: 15)

Against these extreme views at the far ends of the spectrum, we have the view according to which Indian philosophy is not destroyed but captured. Conceding the successful penetration of colonialism into Indian society, Kalidas Bhattacharyya says:

The picture altered, however, with the Britishers consolidating their hold on this country. They somehow captured the Indian mind, primarily through...science (and technology)...and, secondarily...through...the three human values—equality, fraternity, and love... The Indian mind—at least the mind of the mainstream that was Hindu—being thus captured, Western learning found an easy access to this country. (1982: 172)

There is yet another view held by Oxford philosopher Michael Dummett, according to which Indian philosophy is not killed but only 'blanketed'. Dummett says the massive impact of Western culture upon the East has been all the more crushing because political hegemony accompanied the cultural imperialism. 'As a result', he says, 'indigenous traditions have been, not killed, but blanketed... By "blanketing" I mean that the tradition did not die: it was, and still is, preserved... It was being handed down, without alteration, but not being added to; the creativity had gone.'[6] (1996: 14–15)

While the above views use lucid metaphors such as 'mere surface deterioration', 'dead and mummified', 'captured', and 'blanketed', they do not sufficiently capture the picture of Indian thought subsequent to colonialism. Here I would like to reiterate that the first two views, put forth by Sri Aurobindo and Daya Krishna, offer certain conclusions— one offering consolation that nothing significant has changed due to colonialism and the other bemoaning that it is all gone. While agreeing with Daya Krishna's concern for Indian philosophy, it is nevertheless necessary to improvise on his metaphor, as it does not sufficiently capture the complexity. To say that it is 'dead' or 'mummified' is to concede too much to colonialism. While colonialism has largely been very effective, it is not complete; therefore, we cannot conclude that it has left philosophy in India 'dead' or 'mummified'.[7] Even Bhattacharyya and Dummett fail in this regard—to say that it was 'captured' leaves the feeling that it is alive, though in captivity, but that is not what has happened because there is a damage at the structural level. Further, it is not merely blanketed, but structurally altered. That is, none of these views sufficiently succeed in revealing the picture of Indian society after colonialism which has taken on the form of a collision of two civilizations, reminiscent of a head-on collision of two running trains.

To my mind—and I shall substantiate this in the following pages— colonialism did bring about certain major structural changes in the practice of philosophizing in India.[8] It disrupted the relational network existing in Indian philosophy. However, the demolition undertaken was not complete, which is what increases its complexity. It is necessary to take a different view of this incomplete structural demolition. Alternatively, I think the most important achievement of colonial intervention[9] in the Indian psyche is that it disturbed its structure and dialogic tradition. I would like to describe this scenario through an episode from the Hindu epic, *Mahabharata*. Contemporary Indian philosophy has become like Jarasandha's body after he was slain by Bhima.[10] In the fight between Bhima and Jarasandha, the former failed to kill the latter. Each time Bhima severed the limbs of Jarasandha, they magically came together. It was only when Krishna indicated to Bhima how he could kill Jarasandha that the latter succeeded in defeating Jarasandha by tearing him into two and throwing the two parts of the body in opposite directions, which, however much they tried to come together, failed to become one.

Like Jarasandha's torn body, the various parts of the dialogic tradition in India, following the colonial intervention, have never been able to come together again. At best they could only touch each other. In retrospect, perhaps what Indian thought needs today is the compassion of the Rakshasi who brought the two parts of Jarasandha's body to the king. Here the distance is not physical; it is an instance of physical nearness and visual distance. In this study, I shall concentrate on how colonialism seems to have operated on Indian philosophy, particularly contemporary Indian philosophy. The conclusion of this study may be tentatively used to generalize and understand the larger impact of colonialism on Indian society.

Before I embark on my discussion on the different aspects of the partial demolition of the dialogical structure, I would like to point out, through a digression and by way of a flashback, that the civilization that fractured India had also fractured its own pre-modern society. In other words, internal demolishing preceded the external, the former may even be said to be the precondition for undertaking the latter. Hence at the level of intentionality there is invariance. However, there is variance in its success and impact. That is, they did not produce the same results—whereas the West seems to have demolished the pre-modern and built in its place modern institutions, in India on the other hand, the demolition was not complete. Some structures collapsed; in some cases the backyard moved to the front, the interiors were turned upside down, and the house became topsy-turvy. It remained dislocated, the debris was not removed, so it had neither the clarity of the modern West nor of its own nativity. Subsequently, life started growing inside this half-demolished building called contemporary Indian society. To take recourse to metaphor again, the West has amputated its infected arm, but the injured limb of India is still dangling, lacking the clarity of the amputation, as well as the facility of the pre-fractured part of the body. Thus, a dialogical tradition has been 'wounded' *a la* Naipaul. No, this is not a simple wound, it is a fracture, much like the fracture of Jarasandha. Though the demolition is incomplete, let me identify the pockets of its success, elaborate on some internal details of the broken communication, and explicate mediated debates of the half-demolished structures and displaced subjects.

With this background in mind, I had perused the works in and on contemporary Indian philosophy and searched for debates. The picture that emerges is significantly different from what is reported by Matilal about the dialogical tradition in classical Indian philosophy. Let me substantiate my view of this fractured Indian mind.

In the course of these readings, I came across many instances where debates are almost absent in contemporary Indian philosophy. This is notwithstanding the fact that there has been a lot of philosophical activity in India as manifested in works on Western philosophy. During this period there was a significant shift in the philosophical activity from the classical Indian philosophy done in Sanskrit to modern Western philosophy in English. Notwithstanding the volume of this philosophical activity in India, it, however, did not culminate in significant debates. In addition, there were instances where though there was possibility of a debate, it was not pursued.

There are also instances where a debate is conducted addressing the other in an ambivalent fashion. For instance, Sorabji in his article, 'The Ancient Greek Origins of the Western Debate on Animals' (1996), in the context of referring to the philosophers' attitude towards animals, discusses stoics, utilitarians, and Daya Krishna. He names all these thinkers while considering their views. About Daya Krishna, he says:

I shall finish by returning to Daya Krishna's distinction between the metaphysical and the moral issues. Animals are not self-conscious, he said; they only feel pleasure and pain. In place of self-consciousness, the Greek metaphysical distinction was based on rationality. But what I want to stress is that there is not one criterion for just conduct, but many. Self-consciousness and rationality may be superior qualities, but superiority is not the only consideration. (1996: 75)

Having identified these positions, Sorabji refers to all others such as the Stoics, Epicureans, and Utilitarians, but when it comes to Daya Krishna he criticizes his view but does not name him. He says:

Rationality, self-consciousness and kinship are not the only considerations either... What I want to say is that moral philosophers tend to be too one-dimensional. They wish to claim that there is only one thing that matters in just-dealing. 'Is the peacock rational?' ask the Stoics. 'Was there a contract?' ask the Epicureans. 'How will you maximize pleasure or satisfaction?' ask the Utilitarians. 'Is the peacock self-conscious?' But life is not so simple... Furthermore, the list of relevant criteria may need to be indefinitely expanded, as our imagination and sensitivity grows. (1996: 75–6)

When he identifies the Stoics and Utilitarians against their own views, what stops him from naming his compatriot Daya Krishna? Is the omission deliberate or an indication of his reluctance to name Daya Krishna while criticizing his view? Or, is there something that is mediating Sorabji's debate despite his efforts? Here one might brush this aside as a mere coincidence not worth taking seriously.

Similarly, Kalidas Bhattacharyya does not name S.N. Dasgupta while refuting elaborately his criticism of Indian philosophy. Dasgupta in his article entitled 'Dogmas of Indian Philosophy' sums up the dogmas as follows:

> The theory of rebirth, the theory of *Karma* and the theory of *Mukti* may thus be regarded as the three most important dogmas through which Indian philosophy has been made subservient to ethics and religion. (1982: 227–8)

To this he adds 'another dogma that found currency with all systems of Hindu philosophy, viz., the dogma of the incontestable validity of scriptural authority' (1982: 231–2). Dasgupta concludes that philosophy 'which remains for ever encaged within its old bars, may well be taken as dead'. He stresses the need to 'rejuvenate and revitalise' Indian philosophy 'by a critical reformation of the fundamental postulates that have so long been guiding its destiny' (1982: 233).

In his essay 'Traditional Indian Philosophy as a Modern Indian Thinker Views It', Kalidas Bhattacharyya refers to these allegations against Indian philosophy, characterizes them as 'The So-called "Dogmas" in Indian Philosophy', and refutes these charges one by one. He says:

> The last serious charge that is levelled against traditional Indian philosophy is that some doctrines which are ultimately of momentous importance for Indian philosophy and life have just been accepted without serious analysis and examination—accepted either because they have just been in vogue since the hoary past, or entirely on the *ipse dixit* of scriptures (not always the Vedas and often scriptures of lesser credibility). These, for example, are (i)...that there is no freedom...anywhere in any life, (ii) the doctrine that yet this chain can be snapped, with the result that a particular cycle of life will not be followed any longer by another cycle..., (iii) that because there is no freewill anywhere moral action is superficially understood as only what has been socially ordained either by tradition or in authoritative works of higher and higher statuses, ending with the Vedas, (iv) that the traditional Indian theory of punishment has, for this reason, been either preventive or just retributive, (v) that *traditions* and *schools* in Indian philosophy have overdone what was required of them: they have crippled originality and freedom of thought, (vi) that to include testimony as a source of

valid knowledge has been an open, almost criminal, challenge to 'reason' which is so much adored today by 'scientific' minds, (vii) that yet at places and particularly in the entire body of the later-day Indian philosophy—notably in neo-Nyaya and, closely on its heels, in other systems of philosophy—there has been an unnecessary parade of linguistic and other subtleties rendering the whole study into a costly intellectual luxury, (viii) that the traditional Indian philosophy has unnecessarily, and even to the point of unintelligibility, distinguished between self and mind and distinguished concepts like *dik*, *desa*, *akasa*, *parimana*, *duratva*, *antikatva*, etc. which would all pass under the blanket notion of 'space', as in Western philosophy, (ix) that the 'science' it has offered under the head *'ksiti'*, *'ap'*, *'tejas'*, *'marut'*, and *'vyoman'* is very primitive, (x) that Indian philosophy has nowhere developed a detailed psychology of wish, desire, will, impression, imagination, etc. and has unnecessarily, in some systems, elaborated at a great length the concept of 'self-illumination (self-evidence)' of knowledge, consciousness or self, etc. Let us see how far these charges can hold out'. (1982: 200–1)

It is evident from the above that while Bhattacharyya refutes the charges made by Dasgupta one by one he, however, does not name him. I am not making these observations simply with reference to not naming the author, but am alluding to the fact that this is a phenomenon of discounting the other and keeping things anonymous. In order to build up this argument further, let us look at other instances. For instance, there are some debates which are relayed through the outside other. These are about reconstructing classical Indian philosophy while identifying what is central to it. The interesting thing about these contemporary attempts at reconstructing the classical is that they are mediated and relayed through the reference points in the West.

RECONSTRUCTION OF THE CLASSICAL

In contemporary Indian philosophy, we come across three major attempts at reconstructing classical Indian philosophy. The first emphasizes that spiritualism is central to Indian thought; it may be seen in the works of S. Radhakrishnan, R.D. Ranade, Karl Potter, T.M.P. Mahadevan, Ramachandra Gandhi and many others. Matilal and Daya Krishna provide the viewpoint that rationalism is the core of Indian philosophy. Debi Prasad Chattopadhyaya considers materialism as the only living component in Indian philosophy. For the present purpose I shall confine myself only to spiritual and rational attempts.

SPIRITUALISM

Philosophy in India, says S. Radhakrishnan, is:

...essentially spiritual. It is the intense spirituality of India, and not any great political structure or social organisation that it has developed, that has enabled it to resist the ravages of time and accidents of history... The spiritual motive dominates life in India. (1977: 24–5)

Here it is interesting to note that Radhakrishnan disagrees with Christian missionaries.

RATIONALISM

B.K. Matilal and Daya Krishna highlight the rigour in the Nyaya system of Indian philosophy. Refuting Zaehner (1974) who alleged that Indian mysticism lacked the logical rigour generally associated with Western philosophy, Matilal argues that Indian philosophy is logic-centred. Matilal elucidates the rational discussions in the philosophical doctrines of Advaita Vedanta and Mahayana Buddhism, which are usually associated with mysticism. He supports his argument by providing a logical exposition of Nagarajuna's *Vigraha-vyâvartanî* and Sriharsa's *Khandanakhandakhâdya*. He asserts that a review of few points described in either of the above texts would prove wrong the premise that Indian mysticism is characterized by 'vague generalities' and 'naïve beliefs'. Matilal states that these texts were written for intelligent and critical readers, who were expected to examine them dispassionately and rationally. (1986: 118–19)

Here too note that Matilal is disagreeing with Zaehner though there are others in India like Radhakrishnan and Ranade with whom he can negotiate his disagreements and highlight the rational aspects of Indian philosophy.

Another instance of this line of inquiry is present in the works of Daya Krishna. Responding to Karl Potter, who equates Indian philosophy with *moksha*, Daya Krishna states that Potter is wrong as moksha belonged to the 'earliest period when the so-called systems were in their formative stage' (1996: 55–6). Further, considering Nyaya (of the Gangesa and post-Gangesa period), Daya Krishna affirms that Indian philosophy is based on the development of logic from the twelfth to the seventeenth centuries when at least thirty-six known thinkers contributed to the development and refinement of logical thought in Indian philosophy. Daya Krishna does not consider these developments as merely isolated instances, but feels that they are pervasive enough to affect all branches of learning (1984: 65).[11] While the attempts at portraying Indian philosophy as spiritualism centred thrive on differences between India and the West, the attempts at portraying it as rational play on the idea of parity and equality. For instance, in the context of clarifying the definition of philosophy Daya Krishna says, 'Indian philosophical tradition is "philosophical" in the same sense as the Western philosophical tradition is supposed to be' (1996: 15, f.3). Here again we see that Daya Krishna is negotiating his disagreements with Potter.[12]

There are, however, some deceptive exceptions to this. For instance, J.N. Mohanty does disagree with S. Radhakrishnan. He quotes Radhakrishnan who said:

The Western mind lays great stress on science, logic and humanism... For the Hindus a system of philosophy is an insight, a *darsana*. It is the vision of truth and not a matter of logical argument and proof.
[And Radhakrishnan in the same context continues]
    The acceptance of the authority of the Vedas by the different systems of Hindu thought is an admission that intuitive insight is a greater light in the abstruse problems of philosophy than logical understanding.

It is, indeed, [says Mohanty] interesting that in pressing this point about 'intuition', Radhakrishnan discusses a whole list of intuitionists from the West: Bradley, Bergson, Croce, not to speak of Plato, Aristotle, Descartes, Spinoza and Pascal. The only Indian philosopher he discusses in this context is Samkara. (1992: 291–2)

This is a deceptive instance as at one level there is a direct debate between Mohanty and Radhakrishnan, but interestingly the former discloses the latter's preoccupation with the Western philosophers even while making the point in favour of Indian philosophy.[13] Radhakrishnan differs with the Christian missionaries in highlighting the centrality of spiritualism in Indian philosophy; Matilal with Zaehner; Daya Krishna with Potter. The Indian philosophers are like fractured parts that, though very close to each other physically, have been turned topsy-turvy, and are thus unable to communicate with each other. These distances can be very effective in disrupting communication despite physical nearness. Moreover, even while talking to each other, the talking has to be mediated by the external relay station. Thus, the basic features of contemporary Indian philosophy that have been discussed above are: the attitude that shies away from the presence of the other, at times even when one is discussing the view of the other philosopher; discounting the presence of the immediate other; and talking about a domestic view through a distant other.

In addition, let us also look at the contributions of others such as B.K. Matilal who contributed to the discussions on classical Indian philosophy. Matilal's contribution has been aptly summarized by Arindam Chakrabarti, who in his Foreword to the second edition of Matilal's essays in *The Word and the World: India's Contribution to the Study of Language* writes:

Matilal is remembered as the most influential initiator of a crossfertilizing authentic dialogue between Western and Indian, classical and contemporary philosophers. (2001: vii)

Making an exact connection between the spatial and temporal domains, Jonardon Ganeri, in his introduction to *The Collected Essays of Bimal Krishna Matilal: Mind, Language and World* adds another dimension to this engagement. He says:

Matilal's disclosure of philosophical connections is not limited to the conversation between classical Indian and contemporary Western philosophers, but extends to the interaction between the classical philosophical schools themselves. (2002: xix)

Here let me point out that the corpus of Matilal's work reveals definitely an authentic dialogue between contemporary Western and Classical Indian, together with the 'interactions between the classical' Indian 'philosophical schools themselves.' That is, the interactions within the Indian classical schools and the dialogue between the Indian classical and the contemporary Western are the major focus of Matilal's work. Here let me acknowledge another contribution by Matilal, namely, his writings on contemporary Indian philosophers, such as Sri Ramakrishna, Sri Aurobindo, Bankimchandra, Radhakrishnan and contemporary themes that includes sati, the problem of inter-faith studies, peace, the Hare Krsna Movement, nationalism, and orientalism. However, these are marginal to him as his major preoccupation is with contemporary Western and classical Indian philosophies. Further, even within contemporary Western philosophy, his engagement is largely preoccupied with analytical philosophy.

J.N. Mohanty undertakes the other important tradition of the contemporary Western philosophy, namely, the phenomenological and the classical Indian. Carl Olson discusses yet another special branch of

Continental philosophy, namely, postmodernism and classical Indian philosophy, in *Indian Philosophers and Postmodern Thinkers: Dialogues on the Margins of Culture*:

This work proposes to have...an encounter between selected Indian and postmodern thinkers by using a hermeneutical dialogue on the margin between eastern and western cultures. The Indian philosophers that I have chosen represent a number of the major philosophical traditions in Indian culture: the Nikâya Buddhists; the Advaita Vedânta (non-dualism) of Sankara; the Visistâdvaita (qualified non-dualism) of Râmânuja; the Dvaita (dualism) of Madhva; and the Saivâdvaita or Kashmir Saivism of Abhinavagupta.

He, however, qualifies that:

Even though my primary emphasis and focus will remain on these classical Indian philosophers because of their profound influence on the rest of the Indian philosophical tradition, I have also included the twentieth-century contributions of Sarvepalli Radhakrishnan and, to a lesser extent, the philosophies of Sri Aurobindo, J.N. Mohanty, and Daya Krishna. (2002: xi-xii)

As with Matilal, with Olson too the major thrust is between classical Indian philosophy and contemporary Western philosophy. While Matilal negotiates the comparison with analytical tradition, Olson does so with postmodernism. What is evident in all these remarkable scholarly achievements is that the classical Indian and the contemporary Western remain the main focus.[14] This is so even while discussing contemporary themes and thinkers. In this context let me recall that these discussions on comparative philosophy go much beyond the earlier concerns of 'East-West philosophers conference in 1939 [which] dealt in generalities and superficialities and lumped Brahman, Tao, and Buddhist Thusness together...[seeing] the world as two halves, East and West' (Wing-tsit Chan in Larson and Deutche 1989: 5). Laying bare the 'presuppositions, or perhaps biases' of the various volumes that emerged from the East-West philosophers conferences and in the back issues of the journal *Philosophy East-West*, Larson says that there was a 'tendency to favor similarities in comparative work while ignoring or glossing over differences' (1989: 9). The discussions by Matilal, Mohanty, and Olson do not 'simply...suggest...the premature assertion of similarities...' but make a serious comparison to highlight differences. So these attempts do lay bare the 'difference'. However they are largely preoccupied with classical Indian and contemporary Western philosophy while contemporary Indian philosophy remains marginal in these works. My intention in this volume is not only to highlight the differences on which debates are conducted but in doing so to also focus on the nature of contemporary Indian philosophy.

Further, there have also been some conscious attempts, at initiating debate, made by Daya Krishna and M.P. Rege which have been referred to as the 'Jaipur experiment', and 'Rege experiment', respectively.

Jaipur experiment: This experiment tried to make the exchange of teachers between the philosophy departments of Jaipur University and the Sanskrit College in Jaipur city. However, says Daya Krishna, the philosophy teachers' offer to do 'courses in Western philosophy with their [Sanskrit] students...has not been so successful as they do not seem to be interested in what we have to offer.' He adds, however, that the 'other experiment...[where we] try to establish a dialogue with some of the pundits in Varanasi, Calcutta and Pune...' was successful as the pundits there responded creatively (1991: xxiii). It is relevant to note here that this enthusiasm seems to have been short-lived as Daya Krishna himself, subsequently referring to these earlier attempts, said that, 'none of these had really clicked. They were good while they lasted. But they did not generate that feeling of discovery, enthusiasm, and success... They were, to say, abortive beginnings which did not lead to any successful fruition' (1991: xii). So even this conscious attempt did not bear long-term results.

Rege experiment: Later there was another attempt by Rege which resulted in *Samvâd: A Dialogue between Two Philosophical Traditions*. This attempt, according to Daya Krishna, did give rise to some subsequent meetings such as the ones at Sarnath on Nyâya, at Tirupati on Mimâmsâ, at Srinagar on Saivism, and at Aligarh on Islam. Apart from these there has not been much that would translate into substantive philosophical debates. A further limitation was that, like the previous attempts by Matilal and others, here too the discussion was largely between classical Indian philosophy and contemporary Western philosophy and very little was said about contemporary Indian philosophy.

As is probably obvious, the prevalent mode of philosophical discourse on classical Indian and contemporary Western philosophy exhausts all possible domains. This means, contemporary India is a philosophic wafer unless contemporary West is foisted on it. This means, that we cannot even articulate our philosophical concerns, except via the classical Indian and contemporary Western philosophy. There cannot be a more nihilistic view about the philosophical possibility of us as a people facing challenges that call for intensive thought. The ideological implications of such a position will be made clear in the course of the discussions.

Now let me turn to those debates in the contemporary, for instance, the one highlighting the differences between Tagore and Gandhi, described in the collection edited by Ravindra Kelkar, *Truth Called Them Differently: Tagore Gandhi Controversy* (Kelkar 1961). Subsequently attempts were made, for instance by Nandy, to discuss the relation between Tagore and Gandhi differently. Nandy says:

To Tagore, the oppositions could best be handled within the format of India's 'high' culture, within her classical Sanskritic traditions, leavened on the one hand by elements of European classicism, including aspects of European Renaissance, and on the other by India's own diverse folk or little traditions. In his world, modernity had a place. To Gandhi, on the other hand, resolution of the contradictions was possible primarily within the little traditions of India and the West, with occasional inputs from Indian and Western classicism, but almost entirely outside modernity. Consequently, there were often sharp debates in public, as well as private discomfort about what the other represented politically.

Having recognized the difference between Tagore and Gandhi, Nandy immediately seeks to absolve them when he says in the very next paragraph:

When closely examined, however, these differences turn out to be a matter of emphasis. Few Indians have used the folk within the classical more creatively than Tagore. And few Indians have used the classical within the format of the non-classical more effectively than Gandhi. Also, despite being a modernist, Tagore began to make less and less sense to the modern world in his lifetime. He ended as a critic of the modern West and, by implication, of modernity. Gandhi, despite being a counter-modernist, re-emerged for the moderns as a major critic of modernity whose defence of tradition carried the intimations of a postmodern consciousness. (1994: 1–2)

Here Nandy expands the conceptual terrain by including the domain of the reader and notes the differences between Gandhi and Tagore, but he too eventually blots out the differences to bolster unity. At one level, he rightly seeks to remove the differences between Gandhi and Tagore, and I agree with his analysis in this case. However, unlike him I would like to keep the differences alive longer and base debates on them. Nandy, given his preoccupation with highlighting the hybridity[15] or the double in contemporary thinkers, does not take into serious consideration the importance of differences amongst them. The non-availability of the philosophy of difference is one of the reasons for his collapsing the available differences. However, Nandy does highlight the differences between Vivekananda and Gandhi with reference to the former's attempt at masculine Hinduism in contrast to Gandhi's emphasis on the feminine (1995: 215–16). In trying to find more such differences on which debates may be located, I begin with the tendency in contemporary thought to somehow underplay or erase or reduce fundamental disagreements to mere contingencies. This tendency is not only accidental or special but also prevalent in other instances cited here, thus perhaps revealing the larger psychological craving to hide or eventually overcome or explain away the internal differences and highlight the commonalities, a need felt perhaps, within the context of the freedom struggle. In this volume, I attempt to move away from this trend, and in doing so, to bolster the differences not at the level of individuals alone but as representing larger processes at work within Indian society both before and after Independence.

To return to the main line of argument, near-absence of debates or mediated instances of debates in contemporary Indian philosophy is quite different from the classical Indian philosophy as depicted by Matilal. The contemporary picture does not provide a firm ground to rehabilitate the dialogical structure of society. And a dialogical structure is vital for the growth of any society. Moreover, the peculiar feature of contemporary Indian thought is that its pre-modern base has not been completely annihilated, as it was in the West, clearing the debris and establishing new modern relational network. At the same time it is equally impossible to go back to the pre-modern. Both these options prevent society from refurbishing the dialogical structure. Contemporary India consists of a combination of the modern and the pre-modern—neither existing together nor insulated from each other, they are physically closer, each obstructing the growth of the other like two wrestlers. So, though there is a need for debates, there are none. It is this scenario that prompted me to search, if not for debates, at least for spaces where debates may be built. In this venture I found three important areas where there is a possibility of debate, namely, Swami Vivekananda and Mahatma Gandhi; V.D. Savarkar and Gandhi; and Sri Aurobindo and Krishnachandra Bhattacharyya. The significant aspect of these combinations is that at least one in a combination represents the pre-modern and the other the modern. Further, the topics that are covered while discussing these things signify important aspects of contemporary Indian society such as, state and the pre-modern society (Swami Vivekananda, Mahatma Gandhi); religion and politics (V.D. Savarkar, Gandhi); and science and spiritualism (Sri Aurobindo, Krishnachandra Bhattacharyya). Each of these aspects significantly represents a dominant aspect of contemporary Indian society. Though there seems to be adequate ground and resources to retrieve a dialogical network between these thinkers—here it may be noted that they themselves have not made efforts to refer to the other's ideas[16]—these have not been sufficiently highlighted and discussed. The debate between these contemporary Indian thinkers is not relayed like those that have been discussed earlier, nor do they commit the temporal imbalance of juxtaposing classical Indian philosophy with modern Western philosophy, that surrounds the works of Matilal and others. The possible debates that I present here are between two contemporary Indian philosophers on substantive themes which are informed by the classical Indian, and Western traditions of philosophy, the colonial context and the aspirations of an informed, not merely emotive, postcolonial awareness.

In the following chapters I propose to retrieve these debates, bringing into focus what have been dormant, thus engendering debates in contemporary India. This I believe will not only fulfil a long-standing need but also enrich contemporary Indian philosophy. Having presented the three debates in Chapters 2, 3, and 4, in Chapter 5, I shall conclude with a look at the complexity of contemporary Indian philosophy[17] and the nature of the postcolonial self.

NOTES

1. Expressing a similar view much earlier at the social realm, Swami Vivekananda says that:

   ...at the end of the Mohammedan period...an entirely new power made its appearance on the arena and slowly began to assert its prowess in the affairs of the Indian world.

   This power, he says,

   ...is very new, its nature and working are so foreign to the Indian mind, its rise so inconceivable, and its vigour so insuperable that though it wields the suzerain power up till now, only a handful of Indians understand what this power is. (Vol. IV, 1994: 448)

2. An interesting aspect of contemporary Indian philosophers is that while making a case for India in the face of colonial onslaught, they did not either hide or ignore the defects within Indian theories and realities. In fact, their

criticism of the British either immediately followed or even preceded their admission of the internal problems. For instance, see the following statement by Mahatma Gandhi, 'I am against conversion whether it is known as *shuddhi* by Hindus, *tabligh* by Mussalmans or proselytizing by Christians.' The recognition of the internal problems within Indian society is also evident in others like Tagore when he admits that we 'Indians have had the sad experience of in our own past...' (2002: 118)

Here it may be noted that Tagore, while accepting the problems within Indian society, does not embrace the West as an alternative. He simultaneously, attempts to negotiate both the critique of a modern nationalism and the virtues of native societies, along with highlighting the difficulties in native societies. The formulation significantly changes if one looks at only the critique, leaving aside the internal problems. In contrast, if we look at the dissenters of modernity within the West, especially the romantics, there is no such admission of internal problems. Fanon goes one step further and attributes all the problems of the natives to the colonizers. He says:

> Native society is not simply described as a society lacking in values. It is not enough for the colonist to affirm that those values have disappeared from, or still better never existed in, the colonial world. The native is declared insensible to ethics; he represents not only the absence of values, but also the negation of values. He is, let us dare to admit, the enemy of values, and in this sense he is the absolute evil. He is the corrosive element...he is the deforming element, disfiguring all that has to do with beauty or mortality; he is the depository of maleficent powers, the unconscious and irretrievable instrument of blind forces. (*The Wretched of the Earth*, 1977: 32)

This balance maintained by Indian thinkers did concede problems within the indigenous communities and did not attribute all evils to the oppressor. The simultaneous critique of colonialism/modernity, while also focusing on the internal evils within Indian society, becomes one of the unique combinations as well as strategies of the Gandhian political programme. Unlike other social movements, which, while attending to the external oppression, have either neglected or refused to recognize their own attendant problems, or even held their enemy responsible for all the internal evils, Gandhi displayed his ingenuity by simultaneously negotiating them. This balanced nature also becomes evident in J.L. Mehta when he says:

> Those of us who happen to have been born before the eclipse of the imperial Raj and were subjected to the Macaulay gospel and its subtle and pervasive indoctrinative power over the wariest, have much to regret but also much to be thankful for. (1990: 163)

It may be assumed that this difference between contemporary Indian philosophers and others mentioned above would have serious implications for the formation of processes after the departure of the oppressor.

3. Referring to the decline in Sanskrit studies subsequent to colonialism, Sheldon Pollock says:

> ...in most disciplines Sanskrit knowledge proved completely powerless in the face of its colonial counterpart is hardly open to dispute. (2002: 431)

Further, see K. Satchidananda Murthy's *Philosophy in India: Tradition, Teaching and Research* (1985), which discusses some important aspects of philosophy in India, particularly chapter 4, 'Philosophy in Modern India' (pp. 97–115) and chapter 6, 'Problems of the Profession' (pp. 137–56).

4. However, at the social level there were many others who were not as optimistic or practical as Dasgupta. Among them was Rabindranath Tagore who, while being critical of the inundation, alluded to the native forms. Tagore says:

> Before the Nation came to rule over us [under British colonial rule] we had other governments which were foreign, and these, like all governments, had some element of the machine in them. But the difference between them and the government by the Nation is like the difference between the hand-loom and the power-loom. In the products of the hand-loom, the magic of man's living fingers finds its expression, and its hum harmonizes with the music of life. But the power-loom is relentlessly lifeless and accurate and monotonous in its production. (1985: 10)
>
> I am quite sure in those days we had things that were extremely distasteful to us. But we know that when we walk barefooted upon ground strewn with gravel, our feet come gradually to adjust themselves to the caprices of the inhospitable earth, while if the tiniest particle of gravel finds its lodgement inside our shoes we can never forget and forgive its intrusion. And these shoes are the government by Nation— it is tight. It regulates our steps with the closed-up system within which our feet have only the slightest liberty to make their own adjustments. Therefore, when you produce statistics to compare the number of gravels which our feet had to encounter in the former days with the paucity in the present regime, they hardly touch the real points...the Nation of the West forges its iron chains of organisation which are the most relentless and unbreakable that have ever been manufactured in the whole of history of man. (1985: 14)

6. At the social level Partha Chatterjee accentuates this. He says:

> Nationalism has arrived [in India]; it has now constituted itself into a state ideology; it has appropriated the life of the nation into the life of the state. (1986: 161)

Javeed Alam goes one step further in this direction and offers secularism as indispensable to Indian society and he bases this recommendation on the assumption that in India individuation, an aspect of modernity is complete. Notwithstanding the desirability or otherwise of the former view, the factuality of the latter is contestable. I have elaborately discussed the problems associated with Javeed Alam's position in my essay, 'Secularism and Time'. (2000)

7. Yet another reason for rejecting the interpretation of the death of philosophy in India is that the notion of 'revival' is closely related to death. Tapan Raychaudhuri maintains:

> The second reason why the term 'revivalism' is misleading is that it is difficult to revive something that is far from dead. The hold of traditional Hindu practice on the lives of all but a few among the Bengali Hindu intelligentsia was still very strong in the second half of the nineteenth century. (1988: 9)

Here let me reiterate that philosophy in India is not dead but fractured.

8. At the social level Sudipto Kaviraj does talk about an aspect of this structural transformation through the distinction between fuzzy and enumerated communities. But it must be noted that the enumeration is not complete and it will not be allowed to be completed as the fuzzy communities are not mere passive agents and they do contest the enumeration process, which is what gives this process the form of hybridity. Hybridity is not a simple declaration of fact and there is a need to clearly announce the various proportions of this hybridity, which is what is attempted in the following.

9. Here it may be noted that the West does not launch colonialism from an authentic authority. In order to make better sense of this feature it is necessary to initially dissociate the moral and political aspects generally associated with colonialism. For instance, I would contest the view which treats colonialism as predominantly a political programme as held amongst others by Said who sees orientalism as 'fundamentally a political doctrine' (1979: 204). In bypassing the moral question debating whether colonialism is bad or not, or the political question of it being oppressive or liberating, thereby circumnavigating Foucault's formulation of power and knowledge, I, following Ashis Nandy, would treat colonialism as a 'state of mind' expressed in the 'sphere of psychology' (1994: 1–2). However, I would go beyond Nandy and relate the 'sphere of psychology' not merely to the belief in the doctrine of 'progress' as maintained by him but to the developments in cosmology. Let me elaborate.

The rise of Enlightenment individualism cannot be accounted for exclusively by philosophical or social-economic transformations. Perhaps we may find a clue in the coincidental rise of heliocentrism and anthropocentrism—a coincidence, which I think, is not explored in the scholarship—and relate it to the Enlightenment. Thomas Kuhn has suggested that the Copernican revolution though initiated 'as a narrowly technical and highly mathematical revision of classical astronomy became one focus for the tremendous controversies in religion, in philosophy, and in social theory, which, during the two centuries following the discovery of America, set the tenor of modern mind' (1959: 2). This remark allows us to juxtapose heliocentrism and anthropocentrism. As the Earth was removed from the centre of the universe and relegated to the periphery, this lost centrality of man is sought to be compensated by a thoroughgoing anthropocentrism, whereby man becomes the source and the creation of society and its institutions. This compensation seems, even if incomplete and distorted, an existential need indeed! The fall of geocentrism is the precondition for the rise of anthropocentrism, which constitutes the core of modernity.

These cosmological developments seem to be at the back of the emergence of the Enlightenment project which is treated here as a psychological craving for certainty by the displaced subject. Looked at from this perspective, modernity springs from an uncertain terrain, is surrounded by insecurity rather than an assertion of strength, and attempts to overcome weakness rather than issuing out from the strong centre. Its violence is largely the violence of the weak rather than the strong. Unlike many who attributed strength to Cartesian certainty, I would read in Descartes' quest for certainty a sense of insecurity. It is a displaced insecure man's desperate craving for certainty. For me certainty is not a cause but an effect caused by the lost centrality. The cause for certainty may not necessarily be by the agent, who already possesses certainty, asking for more certainty; it may be the insecure displaced self's craving for certainty. In contrast to the mainstream thinkers who established the relation between modernity and tradition, modernity repudiating tradition, I would postulate the relation to be between modernity and cosmology. The former, consequent on displacement, affects the latter, trying to establish at least minimum certainty, embodied in the single letter, the 'I' to begin with, and later extends to other domains, to compensate for the colossal loss resulting from the cosmological developments.

The insecurity of the displaced modern atomized self seems to underlie its attempt to reach out in desperation to the 'other'. Shrouded in this desperation are both the fear of and contempt for the other. This psychological state, to designate to modernity what Said said about the West, vacillates between its 'contempt of what is familiar and its shivers of delight in—or fear of—novelty' (1979: 59). Similarly, to use an observation made by Nandy in a similar context, modernity 'as an ideology can thrive only in a society that is predominantly' non-modern. And, once 'a society begins to become' modern—'or once the people begin to feel that their society is being cleansed of religion and ideas of transcendence'—the political status of modernity changes (1997: 157). In this search for the non-modern 'other', modernity seems to have first encountered its own non-modern and later turned towards the non-Western pre-modern societies, thus paving the way for colonialism.

Given this, I treat modernity as a psychological craving necessitated by cosmological developments. It may be true that the political processes in the form of colonialism ensued from these developments but the internal project preceded and may even be a precondition, like memory in the Bergsonian sense, to its project outside the West resulting in colonialism. That is, the ideals of modernity were first lab-tested and experimented within the West before they were unleashed on other societies.

It springs from a highly charged self-destructive civilization. That is the reason why it is parasitic on the 'other'. The 'other' was first its past, and then it turned towards the other cultures. Nandy says that secularism is always parasitical on the non-secular, West first destroyed and colonized its pre-modern before colonizing the rest. Colonizing itself was the precondition for colonizing the rest. Internal colonialism precedes the external colonialism (Nandy 1997). And for more on this see Raghuramaraju (2005).

Sartre in his introduction to Fanon's *The Wretched of the Earth* recognizes only the external colonialism of the West and not the internal project of modernity.

10. Here let me narrate the story of Jarasandha:

> Brihadratha, the commander of three regiments, reigned in the kingdom of Magadha and attained celebrity as a great hero. He married the twin daughters of the raja of Kasi and vowed to them that he would not show any partiality to either.
>
> Brihadratha was not blessed with a child for a long time. When he became old, he handed over his kingdom to his ministers, went to the forest with his two wives and engaged himself in austerities. He went to Sage Kausika of the Gautama family, with a sorrowful longing for children in his heart, and when the sage was moved with pity and asked him what he wanted, he answered: 'I am childless and have come to the forest giving up my kingdom; give me children.'
>
> The sage was filled with compassion and, even as he was thinking how to help the king, a mango fruit fell into his lap. He took it and gave it to the king with his blessings: 'Take it, Your wish will be fulfilled.'
>
> The king cut the fruit into two halves and gave one to each wife. He did so to keep his vow not to show partiality to either. Sometime after they had partaken of the fruit, the wives became pregnant. The delivery took place in due course; but instead of bringing the expected joy, it plunged them into greater grief than before, for they each gave birth to but a half of a child—each half a monstrous birth which seemed a revolting lump. They were indeed two equal and complementary portions of one baby, consisting of one eye, one leg, half a face, one ear and so on.
>
> Seized with grief, they commanded their attendants to tie the gruesome pieces in a cloth and cast them away. The attendants did as they were instructed and threw the child bundle on a heap of refuse in the street.

A cannibal *rakshasi* chanced upon that place. She was elated at seeing the two pieces of flesh and, as she gathered them up both at once, accidentally the halves came together the right way, and they at once adhered together and changed into a whole living child, perfect in every detail. The surprised rakshasi did not wish to kill the child. She took on the guise of a beautiful woman and, going to the king, presented the child to him saying: 'This is your child.'

The king was immensely delighted and handed it over to his two wives.

This child became known as Jarasandha. He grew up into a man of immense physical strength, but his body had one weakness—namely, that being made up by the fusion of two separate parts, it could be split again into two, if sufficient force were used.

This interesting story embodies the important truth that two sundered parts joined together will still remain weak, with a tendency to split. (*Mahabharata*, C. Rajagopalachari, 1976: 77–8)

Subsequently, there was a duel between Jarasandha and Bhima.

Bhima and Jarasandha were so equally matched in strength that they fought with each other continuously for thirteen days without taking rest or refreshments, while Krishna and Arjuna looked on in alternating hope and anxiety. On the fourteenth day, Jarasandha showed signs of exhaustion, and Krishna prompted Bhima that the time had come to make an end of him. At once Bhima lifted him and whirling him round and round a hundred times, dashed him to the earth and seizing his legs tore his body asunder into two halves. And Bhima roared in exultation.

The two halves at once joined and Jarasandha, thus made whole, leapt up into vigorous life and again attacked Bhima.

Bhima aghast at the sight, was at a loss what to do, when he saw Krishna pick up a straw, tear it into two, and cast the bits in opposite directions. Bhima took the hint, and when once again he tore Jarasandha asunder he threw the two portions in opposite directions, so that they could not come together and join. Thus did Jarasandha meet his end. (*Mahabharata*, 1976: 79)

11. Why is there a need to fix on tradition? I envisage two possible explanations, albeit speculatively:

(a) These attempts at reconstructions of the past seek to re-enact the Western intellectual sequence. Radhakrishnan re-enacting Plato's idealism; Daya Krishna and Matilal, the rationalism of Descartes; and Debiprasad Chattopadhyaya the materialism of Marx. These re-enactments are not true to the original source; they are mediated through the Advaita, Nyaya, and Carvakas, respectively. This, however, does not rule out broad similarities between the Western intellectual themes and the classical Indian schools, stated by contemporary thinkers.

(b) The other possibility is that a specific Western experience, namely, the discontinuity between modernity and tradition that follows the Enlightenment, is sought to be avoided. I have elsewhere argued that the Enlightenment rests on two presuppositions: namely, the hypothetical man (man-in-the-state-of-nature) and artificial society, society as contracted by the pre/non-societal man (Raghuramaraju: 1993b). In doing this, the Enlightenment situated itself outside history, nature, and tradition. This discontinuity leads to a temporal dissonance and ushers in a set of conflicts in the modern West. In India, modernity arrives via the colonial experience. Hence, a temporal dissonance between modernity and tradition within the West in its transplanted context, that is, India, metamorphoses into a spatial disjuncture between the modern West and nativity. Rather hastily, perhaps, contemporary Indian philosophy attempts to overcome the dissonance (a question it need or need not engage with) and this is done by establishing a link between the classical and the contemporary.

In the above, (a) is an attempt to adopt the Western experience, while (b) is an effort to avoid the discontinuities in the West. Adoption and avoidance need not be mutually exclusive; they could be complementary, given the fact that contemporary Indian thought has always been ambiguous towards its experience of the West. In view of this, it should be obvious that the neglect of the Islamic in the contemporary reconstruction of classical Indian philosophy need not be read as a communal stance. In constructing the traditional Indian society as Hindu society, secularist scholarship in India has so far read in this only one aspect of the implication, namely, the communal argument of keeping the Muslims out. Because of this implication they have rejected the entire classical/traditional construction. But one can continue to maintain it, which does not necessarily make this romantic. We can certainly be critical about it, and make these criticisms internal. In claiming them to be internal I am not suggesting that the level and intensity of criticism be toned down. In continuing to maintain the distinction we can recognize that it is only sometimes used by the right-wing organizations to exclude the Muslims and celebrate the past; at times it is also used to make out a case for nationalism. Making this theoretical claim is necessary as the base for colonialism in India was not built through war but on the moral pretext of helping India improve. Given that colonialism is morally justified, there was a need to make a counter moral claim, to show that India had its own civilization. This aspect of the argument needs to be seriously acknowledged. Here it may be useful to remember the good uses of recalling the past as highlighted by Foucault. In an interview with Rux Martin he says that:

> All of this beauty of old times is an effect of and not a reason for nostalgia.
> I know very well that it is our own invention. But it's quite good to

have this kind of nostalgia, just as it's good to have a good relationship with your childhood if you have children. It's good thing to have nostalgia toward some periods on the condition that it's a way to have a thoughtful and positive relation to your own present. But if nostalgia is a reason to be aggressive and uncomprehending toward the present, it has to be excluded. (1988: 12)

12. Here, it must however be stated that Daya Krishna discussed Krishnachandra Bhattacharyya along with Potter and this might go against the view advocated here, that contemporary Indian philosophers are not discussing the issues amongst themselves. Here two possibilities have to be conceded:

(a) The focus of Daya Krishna's discussion remains Potter and Krishnachandra Bhattacharyya is only added to the main argument. Potter is the main contender and Bhattacharyya is a mere surrogate. I draw this inference because it is difficult to envisage the overall thesis of Daya Krishna vis-à-vis Potter, exclusively with Krishnachandra Bhattacharyya. The thesis would have to be restated by Daya Krishna if it is exclusively addressed to Krishnachandra Bhattacharyya.

More substantially, there is a marked difference between Potter and Krishnachandra Bhattacharyya. While the former claims that moksha is central to Indian philosophy, the latter maintains that it is ultimate to it. The term 'central' relegates everything else to the margin and commits more exaggeration than is the case, whereas the term 'ultimate' need not suggest such a conclusion. Something can be ultimate without denying the relative place to others. In this context, moksha may be the ultimate without necessarily relegating or denigrating other aspects such as logic and matter. This subtle distinction has eluded Daya Krishna. If he had taken Krishnachandra Bhattacharyya as a point of reference then the terms of the discourse of his critic would have been significantly different for the reasons already stated.

(b) Another reason for the inclusion of Krishnachandra Bhattacharyya by Daya Krishna is that the latter had already begun programmes in India to promote debates between traditional pundits and modern logicians. This awareness may have prompted Daya Krishna to start the process of talking to other contemporary Indian philosophers.

13. The other exception is the Gandhi–Ambedkar debate briefly initiated by K.J. Shah in his essay 'Dissent, Protest and Reform: Some Conceptual Considerations' (1977) and 'Consensus and Conflict: Some Considera-tion' (1978). Also on the same theme, see D.R. Nagaraj, *The Flaming Feet* (1993). There is also the debate on *purusharthas* by K.J. Shah, R. Sundar Rajan, Rajendra Prasad, and others.

14. It is not surprising therefore to find present day philosophers saying that contemporary Western philosophy may be 'seen to have an underlying continuity with much of classical Indian philosophy' (Mukherji 2002: 934). Mukherji only appears radical when he maintains in this connection

that Indian philosophy was dead long before it was supposed to have been killed.

15. Hybrid system of thought as normally construed about postcolonial thinkers, like Homi Bhabha is saturated and not dynamic. In Indian thinkers one always finds two parts of the hybrid engaging in constant dialogue, and in the process the hybridity itself keeps changing. It is this fact that keeps their thinking from being mechanical, a feature ill at ease with the concept of hybrid. In fact, even the word synthesis which the thinkers themselves might have used fails to do full justice to the richness of their thought texture.

16. Incidentally, in one important respect, *Hind Swaraj* resembles the classical Indian philosophical texts, namely, it is also written in the form of a dialogue with Pranjwan Mehta, an Indian anarchist in England, who Gandhi later identified as his 'dear friend'. Yet another important point is that the two important works bearing the word Swaraj, 'Swaraj in Ideas', and *Hind Swaraj*, are both influenced by Jainism. *Anekantavada* influenced Krishnachandra Bhattacharyya whereas the Jain ideal of ahimsa influenced Mahatma Gandhi.

17. The significance of contemporary Indian philosophy is evidenced by the fact that journals like *Journal of Indian Philosophy* which confined its agenda to the analytical dimension of classical Indian philosophy subsequently had to make room for modern Indian philosophy. This can be perceived in the change in the editorial policy from issues of 2002.

Interestingly, the following clarification by the editor of this journal while publishing an essay on a modern Indian philosopher like Krishanachandra Bhattacharyya, reveals their earlier preoccupation. The editor, while referring to the essay 'Thinking and speaking in the philosophy of K.C. Bhattacharya', by Sanat Kumar Sen, clarifies:

> Although the following essay does not strictly fall within the discipline of classical Indian philosophy, in which our Journal specializes, we publish it here for two reasons: (1) K.C. Bhattacharya was an outstanding philosopher of India in the past generations, and his thought was deeply influenced by his thorough study of classical Indian Vendanta and Jainism, as well as by the study of Kant... (2) His view about the notion of the speakable and philosophy is unique, and it has remained opaque to most of us. Hence some discussion will be illuminating. (*Journal of Indian Philosophy*: 1980: 337)

Thus, this shift referred to above reveals the changes that are taking place not only at the level of teaching but also in the domain of research.

■

CHAPTER TWO

Swami and Mahatma
Paradigms
State and Civil Society

The impact of colonialism on the Indian mind, as claimed by Sri Aurobindo in the quotation cited in the previous chapter, may be confined to mere 'surface deterioration' and it may be 'potentially what it was' thus leaving its foundations intact and unaffected. Despite this, these foundations, however, remain as mere structural embodiments bereft of functional abilities and opportunities much like a partly demolished edifice's weight scattered all over its surface. This is a picture of structural separation between the foundations and the edifice. Even within the edifice there remain many areas which are largely unaffected, while some are partly and others severely damaged. This range, combined with the wide spread across the subcontinent does not make it easy to clear the debris. To complicate this scenario further, some more modern institutions have been introduced from the outside. Alternatively, though the impact is confined to the surface, it may slowly spread to the structures and vice versa. This two-way process between the smashed and the survived on the one hand, and their relation to the institutions subsequently added on, on the other, is interesting to observe. One such coalescing is the interaction between the modern Indian state derived from the West (as argued by Partha Chatterjee) and the communities in India. This is an interesting instance unlike the Western experience where modernity has disinherited its own pre-modern base, walking away as a mere cognitive nude, a state of affairs brilliantly explicated by Descartes. The reality of these nudes could not be denied; at the same time, however, it gave rise to revulsion; clothing the nudes is what preoccupied the Western thinkers later. This disinheritance and the establishment in its place of atomized individuals provided the requisite raw material for the formation of the modern nation-state (see Gellner 1983). This process in India has acquired a different dimension as it did not fulfil the same requirements as of the West and 'their ancestral cultures are not adopted' like the Western nations. The Indian nation-state has to work without atomistic individuals as its foundational resources on the one hand and on the other with diverse communities. Plamenatz elucidates this seminal difference though he does not explain the cost that the Western experience bore. However, it is alluded to by Gellner who felt that the transformation from the pre-modern to the modern is not smooth but violence-ridden. The pre-modern has not resisted this transformation within the West but tamely surrendered to the ideology of the modern. In contrast, in the case of Indian nationalism, the transformation was far less successful, which facilitated an active negotiation between the pre-modern communities and the modern nation-state. In other words, whereas the pre-modern and the modern within the West are sequentially ordered, their ordering in India is simultaneous. However, in India, they coexisted as realities, making their contestation with each other effective and interesting. In other words, unlike in the West, where modernity had a field day in destroying the pre-modern without much resistance from the latter, in India, it was and still is a reality depicted aptly by V.S. Naipaul as 'Hanuman House' in his novel *A House for Mr Biswas* and it does form pockets of resistance. This interesting contrast eludes Partha Chatterjee. Further, and more specifically, it is this success of Western modernity in destroying pre-modern realities that possibly left no choice for the dissenters of modernity in the West but to operate within the realm of fiction like the works of Ruskin, Tolstoy, and other romantic writers. In India on the other hand, the existing pre-modern realities prompted Gandhian dissent to translate into a political programme. Partha Chatterjee makes this point while elucidating the difference. He says:

But the point about Gandhi's selectiveness in picking ideas from his favourite authors can be illustrated a little more in order to lead on to my next proposition that the fundamental core of the Gandhian ideology does not lie in a romantic problematic. (1986: 98)

He goes on to say that the

...thoroughgoing anarchism in Tolstoy was not accompanied by any specific political programme. There was simply a belief that the exemplary action of a few individuals, resisting the state by the strength of their conscience, would sway the people towards a massive movement against the institutions of violence...

In one aspect of his thought, Gandhi shared the same standpoint; but his thought ranged far beyond this specific ideological aspect. And it is here that the comparison with Tolstoy breaks down, because Gandhism also concerned itself with the practical organizational questions of a political *movement*. And this was a *national* political movement, required to operate within the institutional processes set up and directed by a colonial state. In its latter aspect, therefore, Gandhism had perforce to reckon with the practical realities of a bourgeois legal and political structure as indeed of the organizational issues affecting a bourgeois political movement. It was the unique achievement of Gandhian thought to have attempted to reconcile these two contradictory aspects which were, at one and the same time, its integral parts: a nationalism which stood upon a critique of the very idea of civil society, a movement supported by the bourgeoisie which rejected the idea of progress, the ideology of a political organization fighting for the creation of a modern national state which accepted at the same time the ideal of an 'enlightened anarchy'. (1986: 101)

While accepting the distinction made by Chatterjee who relates Gandhi to nationalism through the Western route, I want to emphasize the relation between Gandhi and the pre-modern societies and the critique of modernity, in the process making the necessary route assumed by Chatterjee between nationalism and Gandhi contingent. Moreover, Gandhi's project could become a political programme, a point not recognized by Chatterjee, because there existed pre-modern social realities in India, a facility in a way not available to the dissenters of modernity in the West like Tolstoy and Ruskin, thus forcing their voice to 'lie in a romantic problematic'. Here let me point out that unlike Chatterjee, I would disaggregate 'national' political and treat national only as an aspect of political, and see, again unlike Chatterjee, the political in Gandhi's village reconstruction. To substantiate this, let us see how Gandhi envisages the role of villages even for Europe, not to speak of India. He says:

What may be hoped for is that Europe, on account of her fine and scientific intellect, will realize the obvious and retrace her steps, and from the demoralizing industrialism she will find a way out. It will not necessarily be a return to the old absolute simplicity. But it will have to be an organization in which village life will predominate, and in which brute and material force will be subordinated to the spiritual force. (1968, Vol. 6: 327)

Such a dominant position on villages which does not merely sit in a 'romantic problematic' because there exists pre-modern social realities in India, cannot simply be seen as an instrument for the promotion of the project of nationalism. Here I am not missing the point of Chatterjee's treatment of the problem at the level of its use and co-option by the nationalist thematic and not at the level of Gandhi's intentionality. That is the reason why I am also not making a case at the level of intentionality alone but bringing into focus the alternative thematic of the pre-modern societies as the existing and active realities articulated by Gandhi. So it is necessary to retrace from Chatterjee's fixing of Gandhi as contributor to nationalism to seeing him as the one contesting nationalism, and take the debate between pre-modern and modern into active consideration. The combination that is available in India is the simultaneity of the pre-modern and modern, each in varying degrees in active and passive relation to each other; at times contesting each other; at other times incorporating; at many times just coexisting in an insular manner. Chatterjee, in complaining about the political programme of Gandhi, misses the positive aspects of this difference.

The Gandhian defence of the pre-modern as well as his critique of modernity, and Vivekananda's limited fascination for modernity can become an important starting point to analyse this tension that would help us understand better the dynamics of contemporary Indian society.[1] While Gandhi largely maintained his critique of modernity, Vivekananda, though not an ardent and consistent admirer of the West's modernity, was fascinated by it in the earlier part of his life, though later he denounced his admiration for the modern West. At the age of thirty-five, four years before his death, Vivekananda confessed that his patriotism and zeal as a nationalist reformer were wrong. He declared, 'All my patriotism is gone'. This fascination with Western modernity reflects one of the dominant trends in contemporary India. While this was a transitory phenomenon in Vivekananda, it remains dominant in contemporary Indian society.[2] Vivekananda may have given up his predilection for the West but contemporary Indian society stubbornly and seductively clings to it. In contrast, Gandhi seemed to radically disagree with Vivekananda on this specific issue.[3] These two, namely, Gandhi's disenchantment with the modern West and Vivekananda's fascination for the same, are used here not as views expressed by them as authors but tendencies revealing larger and fast-changing socio-political contexts. In highlighting these differences between Vivekananda and Gandhi I differ from writers such as Sudhir Kakar and Tapan Raychaudhuri who emphasized a state of continuity between the two great leaders. For instance, commenting on the success of Vivekananda's project Kakar says:

The task of fashioning the tools of power with which to effect nationalist aspirations was left for Vivekananda's more pragmatic successors, for men such as Gandhi, Nehru and Patel. (1996: 180)

Here, I would add that Gandhi, who unlike Vivekananda, deplored the pro-modern West bias, also opposed his project. Further, Raychaudhuri evokes the common ground between Vivekananda and Gandhi. He says:

There is something very Gandhian in his [Vivekananda's] rejection of western values... Like Gandhi, too, he is not particularly excited by the varied spectacle of western civilization. (1988: 339)

One could agree with this statement only when one thinks of the later part of Vivekananda's life. Gandhi and Vivekananda held diametrically opposite views on the Western civilization and the Gandhian project cannot be seen as a mere carrying forward of the politics of Vivekananda. Nandy, as already pointed out, clearly highlights the difference between Vivekananda and Gandhi. I must add, however, that in instituting this opposition I am not discounting many areas of commonality between these two thinkers. For instance, Gandhi seems to have derived from Vivekananda that Truth and God are invariant. A.P. Sen points out at another similarity. He says:

...exposure to a wide cross-section of people not only led Vivekananda to appreciate the diversity of Indian life but also paradoxically, the underlying oneness of their material problems. It was evidently on these wanderings that he, for the first time, began to formulate his vision of the Indian mission that in some respects seems to broadly anticipate Gandhian programmes of voluntary education and social work in the vast Indian countryside. (1993: 321)

Further, Sen points out:

Vivekananda anticipated Gandhi in probably two respects one of which surely is the attack on untouchability and human oppression in the name of caste and the other, the idea of voluntary movements and restoring the dignity of human labour. (1993: 289)

While accepting these commonalities I would contest the attempts of those like Kakar and Raychaudhuri who seem to be extending such commonality to those areas where it cannot hold good. My aim is to point out that convergences between the two thinkers seem to have served the political project of the freedom struggle. Now it is necessary, also for a political project of postcolonialism, to go beyond these, identify the islands of difference, and focus on the available active negotiations in contemporary Indian thought. This recognition, in my view, goes a long way in formulating a postcolonial India, which is informed by colonialism and at the same time recognizes, not necessarily endorses, the realities of pre-colonial Indian society.

Now let me justify moving from the individual author to larger political paradigms thus designating these views as the Swami paradigm and Mahatma paradigm. Though Vivekananda and Gandhi have authored these views I would like to see the significance of these formulations in a broader framework. Here I would like to apply Foucault's notion of 'founders of discursivity' to these two thinkers. While referring to Marx and Freud, Foucault says:

They are unique in that they are not just the authors of their own works. They have produced something else: the possibilities and the rules for the formation of other texts. In this sense, they are very different, for example, from a novelist, who is, in fact, nothing more than the author of his own text. Freud is not just the author of *The Interpretation of Dreams* or *Jokes and Their Relation to the Unconscious*; Marx is not just the author of the *Communist Manifesto* or *Das Kapital*: they both have established an endless possibility of discourse. (1984: 114)

Raymond Williams too elucidates this difference when he proposes the distinction between 'indicative' and 'subjunctive' texts. The indicative texts simply show what 'was, or offered to be, an account of what had happened and what was happening' in the world, whereas the subjunctive texts, he maintains, gesture towards a radical normative perspective or impulse 'which is actually not socially or politically' readily available, not even entirely permissible within the prevailing social order (1986: 12). They are always 'attempting to lift certain pressures, to push back certain limits; and at the same time, in a fully extended production, bearing the full weight of the pressures and limits, in ways which the simple forms, the simple contents, of mere ideological reproduction never achieve' (1986: 16).

In this context we may also recall Said who said that texts 'are worldly, to some degree they are events, and, even when they appear to deny it, they are nevertheless a part of the social world, human life, and of course the historical moments in which they are located and interpreted' (1984: 4). Subsequently, in his later work, *Culture and Imperialism*, he maintains that while all texts are 'worldly', and texts or 'masterpieces' encode the greatest pressures and preoccupations of the world around them, they successfully reveal and formalize prevailing structures of attitude and reference and, in so doing, indicate both the possibilities and the limits of these structures.

I too look at Vivekananda and Gandhi as the founders of discursivity. There is yet another difference between thinkers like Vivekananda and Gandhi on one hand and Marx and Freud on the other. These latter thinkers dictated by the necessity of doctrines have shrunk the purview and the range of their contexts. However, Vivekananda and Gandhi are not systematic authors as they were responding to different contexts. Though Gandhi's writings now run into one hundred volumes, only a few of them can be said to be systematic writings like *Autobiography* and *Hind Swaraj*. Similarly, only Vivekananda's works on different yogas can be said to be systematic writings, the rest are in the forms like lectures and letters. So they are not like the 'interlocutor'. Here Said may be of some use. Referring to the 'antiseptic' and 'controlled quality of a thought-experiment' such as 'Bakhtinian dialogism and heteroglossia', Jurgen Habermas's 'ideal speech situation', or Richard Rorty's picture (at the end of *Philosophy and the Mirror of Nature*), he says:

[T]his kind of scrubbed, disinfected interlocutor is a laboratory creation with suppressed, and therefore falsified, connections to the urgent situation of crisis and conflict that brought him or her to attention in the first place. (1989: 210)

In contrast, writes Said:

It was only when subaltern figures like women, Orientals, blacks, and other 'natives' made enough noise that they were paid attention to, and asked in so to speak. (1989: 210)

Unlike the 'antiseptic' and 'disinfected' interlocutors, Vivekananda and Gandhi are more field-level thinkers articulating the popular consciousness which is both dormant and scattered, and responding to tricky situations.[4]

Having explained my movement from the author to the paradigms, let me further clarify my choice of Swami Vivekananda to represent the Swami paradigm. The very first point that needs clarification is why did I choose Swami Vivekananda when the views that he held were formerly held by others such as Bankimchandra Chattopadhyaya. There are indeed studies, situated as it were within the history of ideas—like Partha Chatterjee's *Nationalist Thought and the Colonial World: A Derivative Discourse?*

(1986), which give foundational status to Bankimchandra in demarcating three different important moments—the moment of departure (Bankimchandra); the moment of manoeuvre (Gandhi); and the moment of arrival (Nehru). In Chatterjee's book, the qualitatively different moments are shown to be nevertheless lending themselves to a cumulative programme. In his preoccupation Chatterjee, while acknowledging important differences between Bankim and Gandhi, sets these differences aside and highlights instead the developments within the nationalist problematic. This is because he sees them as belonging to a different temporal order and thereby misses out on the available tension. Chatterjee tamely reduces Gandhi within the problematic of nationalism in the process discounting Gandhi's constructive programme. In doing so, Chatterjee establishes a relation between different nationalist thinkers. However, this lends itself to a contributive-cumulative analysis, and fails to retrieve important differences. While not rejecting Chatterjee's analysis of Indian nationalism, I reaffirm the importance of Gandhi's differences with his predecessors. In a way his criticism of the formation of nationalism in India distracts attention from recognizing the constructive and positive aspects of subaltern communities.

The ascending order, from Bankim to Nehru via Gandhi, in which movements lead to a process, an approach followed by Chatterjee, reveals the story of the success of one process—in this case the dominant process of the 'cunning of reason' through the nationalist agenda, and thereby revealing the tragedy of defeat and disappearance of the non-nationalist social spaces. The overemphasis on or preoccupation in recording or effecting the implication of the tragedy does give the impression that these spheres are ineffective and devoid of political resistance. Such an approach may be viable in the case of the formation of the Western nation-states, as in the West the pre-modern had tamely surrendered to the ideology of the modern nation-state. However, in the case of India, though this approach significantly captures and brilliantly presents some aspects of the formation of the Indian nation-state insofar as it is a legacy from the West, it, however, fails to account for the dissimilarities between the role of the pre-modern in the West and in India. On this count I find Chatterjee's role as the author of this work wanting as a subaltern historiographer and also as a postcolonial thinker. In the present work, therefore, I focus on the non-tragic aspects, which have provided resistance to the nationalist agenda and modernity in India, and follow not the ascending but contesting approach between the processes of modernity and the counters to it from the pre-modern realm. The success of the ascending approach significantly depends on the tame surrender of the preceding stages; in this case the nations in the West could succeed because of the tame surrender of their pre-modern. But if they had not, then that would have put brakes on the ascendancy process, and if the intensity were rigorous it would have turned into a terrain of contestation.

To summarize, the ascending movements are crucial to Chatterjee's approach, and this perhaps may be an appropriate approach used to understand the nation-building process in the West, where the social realities preceding the ascendancy have tamely made an exit. This approach is further used by him to understand nation formation in India which I am ready to concede to a point as it makes a limited and significant point but given the different historico-sociological condition, namely the active pre-modern domain with potentiality for resistance, the ascendancy has to give way to contestation in the Indian context, which is what is highlighted in the following pages. Further, Partha Chatterjee looked for continuity and progressive accumulation of different moments from Bankim via Gandhi to Nehru. In contrast, I see a difference between Vivekananda and Gandhi.

In another important book, *Europe Reconsidered* (1988), Tapan Raychaudhuri discusses three thinkers: Bhudev Mukhopadhyay, Bankimchandra Chattopadhyaya, and Swami Vivekananda. Though the choice of these thinkers and their order in both Chatterjee and Raychaudhuri suggested important insights, such an ordering can also be restrictive. Here I propose to disturb this ordering by choosing Vivekananda from Raychaudhuri and Gandhi from Chatterjee and laying bare two important paradigms.

There is yet another justification regarding the choice of Vivekananda over Bankim as representing the Swami paradigm.

Sri Aurobindo identifies the 'artistic' qualities of Bankim which persuaded him to place Bankim over others such as Rammohun Roy and Vidyasagar. Sri Aurobindo writes:

I do not mean that there were no labourers in the field before Bankim and Madhusudhan...Vidyasagara, though he had much in him of the scholar and critic, and nothing of an artist; Okhay Kumar's audience ran only to the subscribers of a single magazine; and the literary originality of the rest was not equal to their audacity. None of them could transform and recreate with that sure and easy touch which reveals the true maker of language.

Bankim moreover has this splendid distinction, that he more than any one exalted Bengali from the status of a dialectic to the majesty of a language ('Bankim Chandra Chattopadhyaya', Vol. 3, 1972: 95–6).

Interestingly, though Sri Aurobindo finds artistic qualities in Bankim which leads him to hoist Bankim over other illustrious contemporaries, this artistic realm is nevertheless perceived largely as an elitist domain, that prevents Bankim's programme in Chatterjee's reading from taking the shape of a political programme. Highlighting this limitation in Bankim, Partha Chatterjee says:

...the characteristic form of nationalist thought at its moment of departure...leads inevitably to an elitism of the intelligentsia, rooted in the vision of a radical regeneration of national culture. In Bankim's time, the heyday of colonial rule, this vision could not find any viable political means to actualize itself. Instead, it became a dream: a utopian political community in which the nation was the Mother, once resplendent in wealth and beauty, now in tatters. (1986: 79)

The limitation of the literary domain was not a problem with Vivekananda, as he operated with ease and success in the political domain and was also fairly successful outside Bengal since language was not a barrier for him as it was for Bankim. He operated outside Bengal both at the national and the international level and within the political sphere. Referring to the wider political realm of Vivekananda, Sudhir Kakar says:

By carrying within him a sense of his own psychological inviolacy, coupled with a stubborn will that held to the self-chosen course in the face of all outer obstacles, Vivekananda could, when the time came, project his vision with a passionate conviction capable of striking such a responsive chord in his audience that action on a large scale and resistance to the status quo (political and cultural) became possible.[5] (1996: 177–8)

Pointing out the contribution of Vivekananda in comparative terms vis-à-vis his predecessor like Ramakrishna and Rammohun Roy, Hiltrud Rüstau says:

...neither Rammohun Roy nor Ramakrishna Paramahamsa developed a social philosophy proper in the sense of systematically philosophizing on social problems.
　　This was achieved by Vivekananda, who rightly can be named as the first among Indian philosophers for whom social philosophy constituted an integral part of his philosophic system. He was the first who connected his new interpretation of the Advaita Vedanta with the development of a social philosophy

that corresponded to the requirements of a modern society. (1999: 266)

A.P. Sen bolsters this when he says:

...Bankim Chandra never received as much public acclaim outside India...because he never had the occasion to personally visit the West. (1993: 292)

Further, he points out another limitation in Bankim when he says:

Although [Vivekananda's] identification with resurgent Hinduism is in one sense more passionate than that of Bankim, educated Muslim public opinion was less hostile to Vivekananda than it eventually became in relation to the author of *Rajsingha* and *Anandamath*. Evidently as one scholar points out, it was Bankim who situated the Muslim as the historical/political adversary of the Hindu. A few interesting observations may nonetheless be made in passing. It was the sheer power of grandiosity of the Mughal administration in India that impressed Vivekananda more than the preceding four hundred years of Indo-Islamic rule. Bankim on the other hand, as creator of a healthy Bengali provincialism, was prone to be more critical of the Mughals who brought the province under imperial control than of the Turk-Pathan rulers who helped Bengal retain her political autonomy.[6] (1993: 293)

In addition, two important similarities between Bankim and Vivekananda are stated by Tapan Raychaudhuri:

(i) Bankim's acceptance of Western superiority is, however, a central theme in the discussion that follows. It has been suggested that he sought to compensate for the resulting sense of inferiority by identifying one area where India, in his view, excelled, namely, her spiritual heritage. Such a view, promoted among others by the Theosophists and Vivekananda, in their very different ways, did become a part of the intellectual vocabulary in the late nineteenth century India. (1989: 136–7)

(ii) The secular objective of dharma was never very far from Bankim's mind. In looking upon religion and its reform as the road to patriotic ends he is in tune with one powerful school of thought of his days. Dayananda, Keshab Sen and later Vivekananda are all parts of this same tradition. (1988: 154)

Further according to Sen:

It is also quite likely that Narendra was somewhat influenced by Bankim's own writings of the earlier years which not only ridiculed the more irrational components of Hinduism but also tended to measure religion by standards of reason and utility. Interestingly enough, the mature Vivekananda may also have inherited from Bankim, the Hindu counter-aggression *vis-à-vis* muscular

Christianity. It was this polemical aspect to their character that ultimately brought Bankim and Vivekananda to the quest for a personal God and the attempt to give virtue an anthropomorphic form around which a 'national' (in reality a Hindu) ideal may be reconstructed. (1993: 314)

Given this, the relation between Bankim and Vivekananda can be seen as that of a seed and the tree. This is, of course, not to discount Bankim's original contribution.

THE SWAMI PARADIGM

The nineteenth century intellectual climate of Indian society witnessed the advent of modern Western ideas of material progress. Without dogmatically rejecting these ideas, Swami Vivekananda qualified, formulated, distinguished, and contrasted the West from India. This thus provided an updated framework that facilitated the classification of scattered perceptions of the West, India, modernity, tradition, etc. The broad features of this framework entitled here as the Swami paradigm, are:

(1) Celebration of India's spiritual past;

(2) Admission of India's poverty and its material backwardness;

(3.1) Punctuation of the limitations of the modern West's material success—its science-technology, industry, its notion of progress;

(3.2) Acceptance of the material progress of the West—not in terms of its limitation but in positive terms;

(4) And the need to use the models of modernity to eliminate India's backwardness and in exchange give India's spirituality to the West. This, in fact, is the orientalistic framework which equated the West with materialism and the East with spiritualism.

Vivekananda consistently equated India with spiritualism and the West with materialism. And throughout his writings and speeches Vivekananda's reading of Indian society contained two basic features. These were: glorification of India's spiritualism, particularly its past, and especially the Advaita Vedanta. However, he was also critical of some aspects of Indian society.

CELEBRATION OF INDIA'S PAST

In Vivekananda's work we generally come across the following reasons for his admiration of India. These are India's religious pluralism, tolerance towards other religions, and Vedanta meeting the tests of modern scientific reasoning.

Regarding India's spiritual pluralism he says: 'From the high spiritual flights of the Vedanta philosophy...to the low ideas of idolatry with its multifarious mythology, the agnosticism of the Buddhists, and the atheism of the Jains, each and all have a place in the Hindu's religion' (Vol. I, 1994: 6). Regarding the Hindus' tolerance of other foreign religions he says, India

...sheltered the persecuted and the refugees of all religions and nations of the earth. I am proud to tell you that we have gathered in our bosom the purest remnant of the Israelites, who came to Southern India and took refuge with us in the very year in which their holy temple was shattered to pieces by Roman tyranny. I am proud to belong to the religion which has sheltered and is still fostering the remnant of the grand Zoroastrian nation. (Vol. I, 1994: 3–4)

Vivekananda's attitude towards other religions is very ambivalent. He at times shows intolerance towards other religions and at other times displays tolerance towards them. It may perhaps be said that he was not against other religions as much as he was fond of Hinduism or Advaita Vedanta.

All these unique cultural characteristics seem to be internal to India's past. There is, however, another important external test that the Vedanta excels. it meets the present-day test of modern scientific reasoning. Vivekananda says:

The Vedas teach us that creation is without beginning or end. Science is said to have proved that the sum total of cosmic energy is always the same. (Vol. I, 1994: 7)

And,

...the religion of the Vedanta can satisfy the demands of the scientific world, by referring it to the highest generalisations and to the law of evolution. That the explanation of a thing comes from within itself is still more completely satisfied by Vedanta. (Vol. I, 1994: 374)

Further,

...the modern physical researches are tending more and more to demonstrate that what is real is but the finer; the gross is simply appearance...we have seen that if any theory of religion can stand the test of modern reasoning, it is the Advaita, because it fulfils its two requirements. (Vol. I, 1994: 376)

Here it is interesting to observe that rather than the intrinsic features of scientific elements in Advaita, it is his endorsement and even covetous fascination for modern science, though with significant reservations, that seems to have forced Vivekananda to make an ex post facto recognition and identification of similar aspects in the Indian tradition, such as the capacity for 'highest generalizations and to the law of evolution', and recognition of reality as 'finer' and not the 'gross' form which is 'simply appearance'. The comparison was, therefore, not made from neutral ground but presented ex post facto from the present, superimposing the aspect of the present onto the past systems of thought.

EVILS IN INDIAN SOCIETY

Along with the admiration of India's past, Vivekananda does list problems infecting Indian society. These are basically the poverty of the Indian masses, weakness of the Hindu race and the superstitions in Indian society.

He identifies that an important thing that is at the 'root of all evils in India is the condition of the poor'. He holds Hindu priests, foreign rulers, and the Hindu aristocracy responsible for the condition of the poor. According to him, both the priest power and foreign conquest have trodden the poor down for centuries. Finally, the poor of India have forgotten that they are human beings (Vol. IV, 1994: 362). And the 'chief cause of India's ruin has been' monopolizing the whole education by dint of pride and royal authority, among a handful of men. He appeals that if 'we are to rise again, we shall have to do it in the same way, i.e. by spreading education among the masses' (Vol. IV, 1994: 482). Further, he maintains that the aristocratic ancestors in India trod the common masses underfoot till they became helpless, and they nearly forgot that they were human beings. In addition, he writes, they were made to believe that they are born as slaves (Vol. III, 1994:192).

The second important defect that Vivekananda identifies in Indian society is a cultural one. There is too much of '...inactivity, too much of weakness, too much of hypnotism...' in the Hindu race (Vol. III, 1994: 193). This is responsible for the Hindus losing faith in themselves. This made the foreign invasion of India possible. He notes, 'Materialism, or Mohammedanism, or Christianity, or any other *ism* in the world could never have succeeded but that you allowed them' (Vol. III, 1994: 167). And this is because we 'have lost faith in ourselves'.[7] (Vol. III, 1994:191)

The third important defect of Indian society is its superstitions. He says: '[Superstitions] have to be weeded out even on this soil, and thrown aside, so that they may die for ever. These are the causes of the degradation of the race and will lead to softening of the brain'.[8] (Vol. III, 1994: 278)

It is interesting to note that the problems of Indian society that Vivekananda pointed out are by no means meagre. Seriously attending to these would call for major structural changes in the Hindu society. While holding the excessive spiritualism of Hindus responsible for the poverty of the masses, and the passiveness of Hindus, which resulted in their subjugation, he compliments the Muslims and the West for destroying the system of exclusive privilege enforced by Hindus and providing an occasion for the salvation of the poor. He says: '...to the Mohammedan Rule we owe that great blessing, the destruction of exclusive privileges.... The Mohammedan conquest of India came as a salvation to the downtrodden, to the poor' (Vol. III, 1994: 294). Regarding the West, 'Materialism has come to the rescue of India in a certain sense by throwing open the doors of life to everyone, by destroying the exclusive privileges of caste'. (Vol. III, 1994: 157)

And to overcome the submissiveness and passiveness of the Hindu race—to acquire vigour in the blood, strength in the nerves, iron muscles and nerves of steel,[9]—there occurs two suggestions simultaneously in Vivekananda's work, one of them is internal and the other external:

(i) He suggests the need to give up mysticism and de-hypnotize the Hindu race, to move on the line laid down by the sages and shake off their inertia, preach the Advaita aspect of the Vedanta to rouse the hearts of men, to show them the glory of their souls. (Vol. III, 1994: 191)

(ii) He also employs another source to overcome India's material backwardness. That is the need to learn from the West their material progress. Attributing Hindus' ignorance of material civilization as the reason for they being conquered by Muslims, he says:

Material civilization...is necessary to create work for the poor. Bread! Bread! I do not believe in a God, who cannot give me bread here, giving me eternal bliss in heaven! Pooh! India is to be raised, the poor are to be fed, education is to be spread, and the evil of priestcraft is to be removed.... More bread, more opportunity for everybody.... (Vol. IV, 1994: 368).

Sounding more emphatic in offering this latter solution he says that we talk foolishly against material civilization. The grapes are sour. And even taking this foolishness for granted, he retorts how many spiritual people are there in India. He further questions, 'In all India there are, say, a hundred thousand really spiritual men and women. Now, for the spiritualization of these, must three hundred million be sunk in savagery and starvation?' (Vol. IV, 1994: 368). Further, he says:

...when the Oriental wants to learn about machine-making, he should sit at the feet of the Occidental and learn from him. When the Occident wants to learn about the spirit, about God, about the soul, about the meaning and the mystery of this universe, he must sit at the feet of the Orient to learn. (Vol. IV, 1994: 156)

Acknowledging Vivekananda's concern about the poverty of the masses in India, Sri Aurobindo says:

Vivekananda accepted Shankara's philosophy with modifications, the chief of them being Daridra-Narayana-Seva which is a mixture of Buddhist compassion and modern philanthropy. (1972, Vol. 22: 55)

Here let me point out some similarities between Swami Vivekananda and Sri Aurobindo. Regarding the importance and necessity of the West to overcome the problems of India, Sri Aurobindo like Swami Vivekananda, says:

We are to have what the West can give us, because what the West can give us is just the thing and the only thing that will rescue us from our present appalling condition of intellectual and moral decay, but we are not to take it haphazard and in a lump; rather we shall find it expedient to select the very best that is thought and known in Europe, and to import even that with the changes and reservations which our diverse conditions may be found to dictate. Otherwise, instead of a simply ameliorating influence, we shall have chaos annexed to chaos, the vices and calamities of the West superimposed on the vices and calamities of the East. ('New Lamps for the Old', 1972, Vol. 1: 40–1)

Further, referring to the contribution of the West to India, Sri Aurobindo writes:

It is only with the period of European influence, the circumstances and tendencies powerful enough to enforce the beginnings of a new age of radical and effective revaluation of ideas and things have come into existence. The characteristic power of these influences has been throughout—or at any rate till quite recently—rationalistic, utilitarian and individualistic. It has compelled the national mind to view everything from a new, searching and critical standpoint, and even those who seek to preserve the present or restore the past are obliged unconsciously or half-consciously to justify their endeavour from the novel point of view and by its appropriate standards of reasoning.... What it did not do from within, has come on it as a necessity from without and this externality has carried with it an immense advantage as well as great dangers ('The Coming of the Subjective Age', Vol. 15, 1972: 22).

Thus there are two different streams in Vivekananda—the celebration of India's spiritual glory and the acceptance of its material backwardness.[10]

With this background of Vivekananda's views on Indian society, let us see how he equated India with spiritualism and West with materialism. He says:

(i) ...I challenge anybody to show one single period of her national life when India was lacking in spiritual giants capable of moving the world. (Vol. IV, 1994: 315)

And,

(ii) Shall India die? Then from the world all spirituality will be extinct...all sweet-souled sympathy for religion will be extinct, all ideality will be extinct; and in its place will reign the duality of lust and luxury as the male and female deities, with money as its priest, fraud, force, and competition its ceremonies, and human soul its sacrifice. (Vol. IV, 1994: 348)

And Vivekananda while equating the West with materialism admits continuity within Western thought, that is, from the Greek to the modern West. He says: 'The one side, the Greek side, which is represented by modern Europe, insisted upon the knowledge of man...' (Vol. I, 1994: 433). Further elucidating the underlying continuity between the classical and the contemporary in the West which is effecting change in India, he says:

The British idea of expansion and progress is forcing us up, and let us remember that the civilization of the West has been drawn from the foundation of the Greeks, and that the great idea of Greek civilization is that of *expression*. In India we *think*—but unfortunately sometimes we think so deeply that there is no power left for expression... Without expression, how can we live? The backbone of Western civilization is—expansion and expression. This side of the work of the Anglo-Saxon race in India, to which I draw your attention, is calculated to rouse our nation once more to express itself, and it is inciting it to bring out its hidden treasures before the world by using the means of communication provided by the same mighty race. (Vol. III, 1994: 441)

Thus, he subscribes to the orientalist categorization that was actually used by colonial scholarship to justify colonialism in India. Having made the demarcation between India and the West, and unwittingly getting trapped in the orientalistic categories and the colonial design, Vivekananda oscillates between two possibilities:

(i) These differences are arranged on a hierarchy where Indian spiritualism reins supreme and Western materialism figures at the bottom. Vivekananda strongly believes that India should retain its spirituality and reject the Western materialism outright.

However,

(ii) Simultaneously, there is in Vivekananda a recommendation for an exchange between Indian spiritualism and Western materialism. This is not to discount Vivekananda's critique of Western materialism.

He warns 'The whole of Western civilization will crumble to pieces in the next fifty years if there is no spiritual foundation'. (Vol. III, 1994: 159)

And,

No nation can be said to have become civilized only because it has succeeded in increasing the comforts of material life by bringing into use lots of machinery and things of that sort. The present-day civilization of the West is multiplying day by day only the wants and distresses of men. On the other hand, the ancient Indian civilization, by showing people the way to spiritual advancement, doubtless succeeded, if not in removing once for all, at least in lessening, in a great measure, the material needs of men. (Vol. VI, 1994: 462-3)

Further,

From the Orient came the voice which once told the world that if a man possesses everything that is under the sun and does not possess spirituality, what avails it? This is the oriental type; the other is the occidental type. (Vol. IV, 1994: 155)

The broad feature of his recommendation is that the exchange between Western materialism and Indian spiritualism is mutually beneficial. He admits that 'Too early religious advancement of the Hindus and that superfineness in everything which made them cling to higher alternatives, have reduced them to what they are. The Hindus have to learn a little bit of materialism from the West and teach them a little bit of spirituality' (Vol. VI, 1994: 115). He also says:

...just as the too active Western mind would profit by an admixture of Eastern introspection and the meditative habit, so the Eastern would benefit by a somewhat greater activity and energy. (Vol. I, 1994: 383)

Elsewhere, he specifies the elements to be exchanged. As he says: 'We should learn from the West her arts and her sciences...the sciences of physical nature, while on the other hand the West has to come to us to learn and assimilate religion and spiritual knowledge' (Vol. III, 1994: 443). This exchange is desirable and without such an exchange each of the civilizations would remain incomplete. He complains that to '...care only for spiritual liberty and not for social liberty is a defect, but the opposite is a still greater defect. Liberty of both soul and body is to be striven for' (Vol.VI, 1994: 86). When each assimilates the other, the ideal would be achieved. 'I would say, the combination of the Greek mind represented by the external European energy added to the Hindu spirituality would be an ideal society for India'. (Vol. V, 1994: 216)

Further, he writes:

India has given to antiquity the earliest scientific physicians, and according to Sir William Hunter, she has even contributed to modern medical science by the discovery of various chemicals and by teaching you how to reform misshapen ears and noses. Even more it has done in mathematics, for algebra, geometry, astronomy, and the triumph of modern science –mixed mathematics—were all invented in India, just so much as the ten numerals, the very cornerstone of all present civilization, were discovered in India, and are in reality, Sanskrit words.

And now, what has the world given to India in return for all that? Nothing but nullification...and curse and contempt.... But India is not afraid. It does not beg for mercy at the hands of any nation. Our only fault is that we cannot fight to conquer, but we trust in the eternity of truth. (Vol. II, 1994: 511–2)

In an interesting passage he remarks:

Why are we so backward nowadays? Why are ninety-nine per cent of us made up of entirely foreign ideas and elements? This has to be thrown out if we want to rise in the scale of nations. If we want to rise, we must also remember that we have many things to learn from the West... We Hindus must believe that we are the teachers of the World... So, I must call upon you to go out to England and America, not as beggars but as teachers of religion. The law of exchange must be applied to the best of our power. If we have to learn from them the ways and methods of making ourselves happy in this life, why, in return, should we not give them the methods and ways that would make them happy for all eternity?

Above all, work for the good of humanity. (Vol. III, 1994: 443–4)

Emphasizing on practicality as the important requirement he says that the need of the people of India is not more religion, but, 'practicality'. In this context it is relevant to recall that he, like a true liberal, places liberty as the first condition of growth. He says, 'Just as man must have liberty to think and speak, so he must have liberty in food, dress, and marriage, and in every other thing, so long as he does not injure others'. (Vol. IV, 1994: 367–8)

Further, regarding the Indians' capacity to adopt European values he says that they cannot wholly adopt as:

With us, the prominent idea is Mukti; with the Westerners, it is Dharma. What we desire is Mukti; what they want is Dharma... However, the central fact is that the fall of our country, of which we hear so much spoken, is due to the utter want of this Dharma. If the whole nation practices and follows the path of moksha, that is well and good; but is that possible? Without enjoyment, renunciation can never come; first enjoy and then you can renounce. Otherwise, if the whole nation, all of a sudden, takes up Sanyasa, it does not gain what it desires, but it loses what it had into the bargain—the bird in the hand is fled, nor is that in the bush caught. (Vol. V, 1994: 446–7)

Further reinforcing this difference he says:

The Greeks sought political liberty. The Hindus have always sought spiritual liberty. Both are one-sided. The Indian cares not enough for national protection or patriotism, he will defend only his religion; while with the Greeks and in Europe...the country comes first. (Vol. VI, 1994: 86)

And this is:

By preaching the profound secrets of the Vedanta religion in the Western world, we shall attract the sympathy and regard of these mighty nations, maintaining for ever the position of their teacher in spiritual matters, and they will remain our teachers in all material concerns. The day when, surrendering the spiritual into their hands, our countrymen would sit at the feet of the West to learn religion, that day indeed the nationality of this fallen nation will be dead and gone for good. Nothing will come of crying day and night before them... When there will grow a link of sympathy and reward between both nations by this give-and-take intercourse, there will then be no need for these noisy cries. (Vol. VI, 1994: 448-9)

In endorsing the possibility and the desirability of exchange between India and the West, Vivekananda is quick to set the terms of exchange. First, the exchange must be on equal terms. He says:

We have been clamouring here for getting political rights and many other such things. Very well. Rights and privileges and other things can only come through friendship, and friendship can only be expected between two equals. When one of the parties is a beggar, what friendship can there be? It is all very well to speak so, but I say that without mutual co-operation we can never make ourselves strong men. (Vol. III, 1994: 443-4)

Second, the exchange must be internally necessitated not externally thrust or imposed. He writes:

...it must always be *we* who build up a new India as an effect and continuation of her past, assimilating helpful foreign ideas wherever they may be found. Never can it be *they*; growth must proceed from within. All that England can do is to help India to work out her own salvation. (Vol. V, 1994: 198)

Finally, the exchange should not be excessive. He says that we must learn many things from the West but:

...there are fears as well... The spell of imitating the West is getting such a strong hold upon you that what is good or what is bad is no longer decided by reason, judgment, discrimination or reference to the Shastras. (Vol. IV, 1994: 477-8)

However, at one place he sounds as if he is saying that the exchange between India and the West is inevitable. He writes:

As Western ideas of organization and external civilization are penetrating and pouring into our country, whether we will have them or not, so Indian spirituality and philosophy are deluging the lands of the West. None can resist it, and no more can we resist some sort of material civilization from the West. A little of it, perhaps, is good for us, and a little spiritualization is good for the West; thus the balance will be preserved. (Vol. III, 1994: 171)

Here for our present purpose, three important features of the Swami paradigm may be stated.

(i) It subscribes to the orientalist categorization that identifies East with spiritualism and West with materialism.
(ii) The Swami paradigm constructs West as a monolith admitting the continuity from Greeks to the present Europe.

(iii) Alongside critiquing the materialism of the West, the paradigm recommends an exchange with the West which would bring materialism to India and help the country to overcome its material backwardness.

THE MAHATMA PARADIGM

Many nationalists and contemporary Indian thinkers have unwittingly or otherwise subscribed to the Swami framework. Though Vivekananda himself seems to have given it up later in his life, this trend has become a dominant force in contemporary India. In such a sense, this framework is paradigmatic.

To my mind, the Swami framework was clearly rejected by Mahatma Gandhi, despite his personal admiration for Vivekananda. However, this rejection of Vivekananda by Gandhi has not been taken seriously. This rejection and the element of difference constituting this rejection are particularly important as these can facilitate a clear exposition of two important contrary positions prevalent in contemporary India. I shall in the following pages seek to bring Gandhi's critique of modernity face-to-face with Vivekananda's admiration for modernity and materialism. Gandhi unequivocally denounced modernity, its technology, and industry. Describing the modern Western civilization as 'satanic' he said that it was bad not only for India, but equally so for the West. And to Gandhi, Indian poverty is the creation of modern industry. So, obviously modernity cannot be used to eradicate Indian poverty. In this context, the Mahatma paradigm is outside the orientalistic framework.

Unlike Vivekananda who subscribed to the orientalistic categorization of identifying India with spiritualism and the West with materialism, Gandhi succeeded in overcoming the problem. In fact, he cast it aside. Instead, he disaggregated the West by introducing a more radical and novel distinction between the modern Western civilization and Western society. He wrote that he 'bears no enmity towards the English but [he does] towards their civilization' (1989: 92). Gandhi acknowledged the use of modern and Western interchangeably. In this regard he says: '...I have so often written and spoken upon and against the materialistic tendency of modern civilization—I will not say Western civilization though as it so happens for the time being, the two have become convertible terms' (1986: 312).

He clarified that modern civilization was different from Western civilization:

Do not for one moment consider that I condemn all that is Western. For the time being I am dealing with the predominant character of modern civilization, do not call it Western civilization, and the predominant character of modern civilization is the exploitation of the weaker race of the earth. The predominant character of modern civilization is to dethrone God and enthrone Materialism. (1986: 345)

He further added:

[The English] are enterprising and industrious, and their mode of thought is not inherently immoral. Neither are they bad at heart. I therefore respect them. Civilization is not an incurable disease, but it should never be forgotten that the English people are at present afflicted by it. (1989: 34)

He maintained:

It is my deliberate opinion that India is being ground down, not under the English heel, but under that of modern civilization. (1989: 38)

Identifying the elements in modern Western civilization he wrote:

Western civilization is material, frankly material. It measures progress by the progress of matter—railways, conquest of disease, conquest of the air... No one says, 'Now the people are more truthful or more humble.' I judge it by my own test and I use the word 'Satanic' in describing it... The essential of Eastern civilization is that it is spiritual, immaterial. (1986: 328)

Further, he wrote:

I do not believe that multiplication of wants and machinery contrived to supply them is taking the world a single step nearer its goal... I wholeheartedly detest this mad desire to destroy distance and time, to increase animal appetites and go to the ends of the earth in search of their satisfaction. If modern civilization stands for all this, and I have understood it to do so, I call it Satanic. (*Young India*, 17 March 1927: 83)

He conclusively asserted that it is 'machinery that has impoverished India. It is difficult to measure the harm that Manchester has done to us. It is due to Manchester that Indian handicraft has all but disappeared' (1989: 82). Making evident a sharp discord with Vivekananda, Gandhi, though without naming him, declared that, 'If India copies England, it is my firm conviction that she will be ruined' (1989: 31).[11] Yet another important difference between Vivekananda—along with many others who have toed the orientalist categorization of the East as spiritual and West as material—and Mahatma is that the latter steps outside orientalistic thematic by disaggregating the West into the modern and the pre-modern.

Gandhi offered a clear critique of modernity. He indicted modern civilization on moral grounds. This civilization, he said 'is irreligious', and it 'leaves no time for contemplation, offers neither stability nor certainty, is treacherously deceptive, hypnotic and self-destructive.' The criticism was clear, forthright and total.[12]

Through this distinction between the modern and British, Gandhi not only highlighted the colonial domination of India by the British, but also emphasized the damage that the modern civilization had done to the Western society. Through this distinction between modernity and the pre-modern, Gandhi managed a stronger criticism of the British rule in India. Modernity not only subjugated the non-Western societies but also subjugated Western society. In other words, modernity brought forth the process of colonization both within and outside the Western society. Through this formulation, Gandhi exposed the expansionism of the British along with instances of internal erosion or derangement caused by modernity within the Western society itself. This reading of modernity helped Gandhi to grasp the qualitative difference between traditional and modern forms of oppression.

Thus, Gandhi disaggregated the West into modern and the non-modern, and noted the similarities between India and the non-modern West. Regarding this he wrote:

The People of Europe, before they were touched by modern civilization, had much in common with the people of the East; anyhow, the people of India and, even today, Europeans who are not touched by modern civilization are far better able to mix with the Indians than the offspring of that civilization. (1986: 293)

To further understand the differences between the approaches adopted by Vivekananda and Gandhi, it may be noted here that while Vivekananda focused on the material backwardness and poverty of Indians and looked for solutions in Western materialism, thereby suggesting the possibility of contact between India and the West, Gandhi concentrated on the moral perils of the people of Europe subsequent to their contact with modernity. It was those Europeans 'who are not touched by modern civilization' that Gandhi felt would serve as a link between Europe and India.

He further added:

East and West can only and really meet when the West has thrown overboard modern civilization, almost in its entirety. They can also seemingly meet when

East has also adopted modern civilization. But that meeting would be an armed truce, even as it is between, say, Germany and England, both of which nations are living in the Hall of Death in order to avoid being devoured, the one by the other. (1986: 293)[13]

Unlike Vivekananda who bemoaned the fact that there was too much of 'inactivity', 'too much of weakness' in the Hindu race, Gandhi, in contrast, said,

There is a charge laid against us that we are lazy people and that Europeans are industrious and enterprising. We have accepted the charge and we therefore wish to change our condition. Hinduism, Islam, Zoroastrianism, Christianity and all other religions teach that we should remain passive about worldly pursuits and active about godly pursuits. (1989: 38)

To further focus on the ignorance of the orientalist construction of the Orient he added:

Macaulay betrayed gross ignorance when he labelled Indians as being practically cowards. They never merited the charge.... Have you ever visited our fields? I assure you that our agriculturists sleep fearlessly on their farms even today; but the English and you and I would hesitate to sleep where they sleep (1989: 40).

To contest the claim that Europeans were known for their unity, which for many including Vivekananda had become a sore point, Gandhi said:

We were one nation before they [British] came to India... I do not wish to suggest that because we were one nation we had no differences, but it is submitted that our leading men travelled throughout India either on foot or in bullock-carts. They learned one another's languages and there was no aloofness between them...they saw that India was one undivided land so made by nature. They, therefore, argued that it must be one nation (1989: 42–3).

The broad features of the Mahatma paradigm, therefore, are: (i) It identifies the modern West with materialism and the non-modern West and India with religion and morality. (ii) It rejects modern Western materialism, thus foreclosing the possibility of any exchange between the modern West and India. Thus the Mahatma paradigm radically differs from the Swami paradigm on important counts.

(1) Vivekananda saw continuity from the Greeks to modern Europe freezing the dynamic feature of European history. He thus endorsed homogeneity and continuity within the West. And, he maintained the difference between India and the West on cultural terms.

In contrast, Gandhi recognized important discontinuities between the modern and the non-modern (or traditional which includes non-elitist society and its institutions), and thus disaggregated the West into modern and the non-modern.

In talking about the traditional West, Vivekananda mostly referred to the Greeks. Gandhi, on the other hand, referred to Christ and the Sermon on the Mount, while talking about the non-modern West. Thus, while Vivekananda subscribed to the orientalist categorization of East with spiritualism and West with materialism, it is in Gandhi that we find orientalism rejected.

(2) Vivekananda recognized the positive aspects in materialism, and recommended materialism to India on an exchange basis for the eradication of poverty and backwardness of Indian society. Gandhi completely rejected modern civilization as satanic and irreligious. For him it was the industry of the modern civilization, its greed for power that created Indian poverty. So it could not be used to eradicate what it has created. Taking a very clear stand he wrote:

Our leaders say that, in order to fight the West, we have to adopt the ways of the West. But please rest assured that it will mean the end of Indian civilization. India's face is turned away from your modern trend; that India you do not know. I have travelled much and so come to know the mind of India and I have discovered that it has preserved its faith in its ancient civilization. The *swaraj* of which we hear will not be achieved the way we are working for it. The Congress League Scheme, or any other scheme which is even better, will not get us *swaraj*. We shall get *swaraj* through the way in which we live our lives. It cannot be had for the asking. We can never gain it through copying Europe. (1986: 302-2)

Gandhi is more radical when he says that modern civilization is bad not only for India but also for the West, displaying in the process his ingenuity in avoiding provincialism. To pick up the thread from the discussions at the beginning of the chapter, there exist both modern and pre-modern institutions in India. The modern may be seen to be consisting of the Indian state and represented by Vivekananda, and the pre-modern consisting of communities and villages represented by Gandhi.

Before pointing out the reality status of the pre-modern in India, let me make some clarifications. It is necessary to recognize that in the West, modernity has destroyed its pre-modern social realities which made Anthony Giddens declare that the only option left is to claim them through the 'sociological imagination', (1982: 14), or through 'art, literature, language, and the cultural "artefacts" of the era in question', namely, the 'pre-modern experience' (Susan Bordo: 1987: 29). Bordo explicitly thematizes this when she says that, 'Although we cannot *experience* the world of pre-Modernity, (as it is no longer our own) we can reconstruct it in the imagination: (Bordo 1987: 29). That is possibly the reason why Foucault suggests the need to conflate 'pre-modern' and 'postmodern', as 'countermodernity' reducing them to be contrasted with 'modernity'. This need candidly captured the changed configurations in the West (1984: 39). However, as explicated before, such a sequence of events may not be applied to India. There is, therefore, a need to correct the political grammar of tense and not use the past tense to designate the living present. This is perhaps the reason why unlike in the West the state in India did not always succeed in coercing social communities. This difference can be deciphered from the following observation from Madan, who says that,

...Nehru's refusal (or failure) to use the coercive powers of the state in hastening this process. In this regard he invites comparison with Lenin and Ataturk... It must be admitted here that the pluralistic situation which Nehru and the other framers of the Constitution faced was immensely more complex than anything that Lenin, and far less Ataturk, faced; yet the fact remains that Nehru did not use his undoubted hold over the people as a leader of the freedom movement and his vast authority as the head of government to bring communal tendencies under strict control. (Madan 1999: 406–7)

Here let me point out that Nehru did not, rather he could not, coerce, which was more a political retreat rather than an individual choice, and this was necessitated by the presence of pre-modern social realities. While pre-modern social realities continue to exist in India, urban India talks about them in the past tense. Pointing this out, Nandy says:

Many living communities are 'dead' in academic texts and in public documents in the Southern world; policy-makers and scholars talk about them in the past tense even when they are a few feet away, perhaps just on the other side of the road. We exile these communities to history, so that we can safely bemoan their death, and thus dismiss all who remain concerned with them as incurable romantics. (2001: 4)

The underside to this deliberate non-recognition is the blind following of the process of modernity in the West, where the pre-modern communities have been successfully erased. Further, in these days of globalization, we do have data to show large spaces of India not affected by it.

Let me elucidate the nature and also the scale of this combination, between the modern and the pre-modern. The following figures might provide a clue to the existing proportion between the modern and the pre-modern in India. Hindustan Lever Ltd.:

has more than 70 per cent share in the shampoo segment but that translates into just about '8 per cent of hair washes'. Ditto with soaps. Two out of every three soaps sold are HLL brands. But only 20 per cent of the people who bathe use soaps. (*India Today*, Nov. 19, 2001: 69)

Further,

Barely a tenth of the milk sold in India is packaged. (Ibid.: 71)

This data from the encroaching other surely is an important description of the existence of the pre-modern communities.[14] Perhaps Tagore captured this ambivalence most succinctly when he says:

I was born in what was once the metropolis of British India... Though the trampling process was almost complete around me, yet the wailing cry of the past was still lingering over the wreckage... It seems that the sub-conscious remembrance of a primeval dwelling-place, where, in our ancestor's mind, were figured and voiced the mysteries of the inarticulate rocks, the rushing water and the dark whispers of the forest, was constantly stirring my blood with its call. (2002: 170–2)

Thus, pre-modern communities and modern institutions exist simultaneously in India. Having maintained the present continuity of the plural communities in India, let me further point out that unlike the oft-made allegation that Gandhi's views are utopian I would maintain that one of his main contributions to social theory is the adherence to a realistic account of community life.[15] Further, these communities are not isolated from each other; at the same time they may not interact with each other regularly. Let me in the following paragraphs discuss the possibility of their interaction and internal preoccupation.[16]

Each community has an internal preoccupation and it provides to its members a vision of the world, and a relation with the past and the future. Critiquing the culture is largely an internal preoccupation. Each community further has an external axis to interact with and visit other cultures. The facility to visit is not an obsession as they are not preoccupied with the world views of other cultures, nor are they obsessed with the others' presence. Here let me distinguish between different kinds of interactions.

(a) A culture can interact with the context of other cultures out of curiosity or to learn from their experience. When one criticizes or rejects another's cultural context, it can give rise to communal conflict. This is what really happens in many cases, for instance, the controversy regarding different civil codes in India. In a similar vein, this is why the idea of conversion conflicts with Gandhi's world view.

(b) There is also the possibility of one context meeting another community's universal and vice versa. Evaluating one community's universal from another community's context is like reading only the literal meaning in a metaphor. And evaluating a universal from the standpoint of a context or vice versa is to commit a category mistake. Even here there is, therefore, possibility of conflict. For instance, Gandhi did not have conflict with Christianity because he found no conflict between the universals of Hinduism as he perceived them and the universals of Christianity. Sufis adopted analogous view vis-à-vis Vedantic Hinduism. Gandhi or Sufis hardly bothered about the varying contexts. But the same cannot be said about orthodoxy of any religion attacking other religion.

(c) Ideally speaking, an interaction between universals of two communities or more and looking at others' contexts through their universals can facilitate a meaningful interaction among communities. One possible mode of visiting other cultures is visualized by J.L. Mehta through the concept of pilgrimage, *tirtha*. The attitude of one community towards the other is like pilgrimage. Krishnachandra Bhattacharyya shows that when the universal of one community moves closer to the universal of the other community, it is possible that it moves farther away from the universal of the third community. He also noted in the context of different religious experiences that the universals of different communities could never be transformed into a single unitary form. Gandhi emphasized the reverence towards other cultures and not criticism and rejection. I reproduce in the form of long quotations from J.L. Mehta, Krishnachandra Bhattacharyya and Gandhi that would throw more light on the nature and interaction of plural cultures.[17]

Mehta puts forward a novel idea of pilgrimage as a basis for cross-cultural understanding and coexistence. He pleads with us to set aside for the moment learned and bookish models for religious understanding, and suggests the model of a pilgrimage as more appropriate and helpful. 'Imagine a group of people, rich and poor,' says Mehta,

...of various classes, coming from different cultural regions of the country, speaking different languages, not necessarily belonging to an identical religious sect, coming together at the starting point of the pilgrimage and venturing forth together on a perilous journey on foot to a common destination, to a major *tirtha* in India up in the Himalayas... Recognizing and respecting these differences, they yet arrive at an understanding which goes deeper than words... What is understanding among people worth if it does not take place in full awareness of our common mortality, common yet beckoning to each of us to meet it alone, in the privacy of our solitary pilgrimages?... Not until living itself is transformed into a pilgrimage, which is nothing if not living in the face of death—one's own—does scripture disclose its sovereign majesty, become truly scripture. (1990a: 93–5)

There is another interesting suggestion in Krishnachandra Bhattacharyya. In his article, 'The Concept of Philosophy', he states:

Religious experience as consciousness of being is simple and admits of no variation within itself. There is, however, an infinite plurality of unique religious experiences. Their relation is determined by themselves and not by any external reflection. Each experience by its self -deepening gets opposed to or synthesised with other experiences. One experience may enjoy another as a stage outgrown or as in absolute conflict with it, where a third experience may emerge as adjusting them to one another. There is no possibility of systematising them by secular reason and so far as they systematise themselves, they present themselves in many alternative systems... The Hegelian notion of a single and exclusive gradation of religions would appear from this standpoint to be intrinsically irreligious...

Religions may indefinitely multiply and indefinitely get synthesised. So is there [sic] indefinite scope for differences and syntheses in philosophical theory in general. There is no question of philosophy progressing towards a single unanimously acceptable solution. All philosophy is systematic symbolism and symbolism necessarily admits of alternatives. (1983: 477)

Mahatma Gandhi seems to be throwing a different light on pluralistic societies in his reply to a letter. I reproduce both the letter and Gandhi's reply.

A Mussulman friend writes:

You regard Mohammed as a Prophet of God and hold him in high regard. You have even publicly spoken of him in the highest terms. I have heard and even seen reports in cold print to the effect that you have studied the Quran itself. All this, I must confess, has puzzled me. I am at a loss to understand how a person like you, with all your passion for truth and justice, who has never failed to gloze over a single fault in Hinduism or to repudiate as unauthentic the numerous corruptions that masquerade under it, can holus-bolus accept all that is in the Quran.

Gandhi's reply:

I have nowhere said that I believe literally in every word of the Quran, or, for the matter of that, of any scripture in the world. But *it is no business of mine to criticize the scriptures of other faiths, or to point out their defects* [Emphasis mine]. It is and should be, however, my privilege to proclaim and practise the truths that there may be in them... But I welcome every opportunity to express my admiration for such aspects of his life as I have been able to appreciate and understand. As for things that present difficulties, I am content to see them through the eyes of devout Mussulman friends, while I try to understand them with the help of the writings of eminent Muslim expounders of Islam. It is only through such a reverential approach to faiths other than mine that I can realize the principle of equality of all religions. But it is both my right and duty to point out the defects in Hinduism in order to purify it and to keep it pure. (1950: 275–6)

These above voices divulge some important shades of the way of life of plural society. Mehta's model of a pilgrimage, Krishnachandra Bhattacharyya's notion of an alternative, and Gandhi's reverence for other faiths reveal different ways of looking at communities. This is qualitatively different from the fashionable views like removing cultural differences or merely tolerating other communities. The plural world views of cultures and communities may not give us a grand social theory but it would facilitate a meaningful co-existence between communities.

The negotiation between these plural communities on the one hand and the modern nation-state on the other, which is a source of a larger debate as seen in the works of Vivekananda and Mahatma Gandhi, would reveal a better understanding of the political processes of contemporary India. But this has eluded the scholars' attention since long. Thus we have in the Swami and the Mahatma paradigms two radically different perceptions. One way of understanding the underlying tensions within contemporary Indian society is to recognize the workings of these two streams. One useful way of retrieving this tension today is to formulate Swami paradigm as being very close near to the nationalist programme and the Indian state.[18] The Mahatma paradigm is closer to the non-state social realities of Indian society. Sunderlal Bahuguna, Baba Amte, and the anti-arrack movement in Andhra Pradesh embody some of the visible aspects of India's non-state societal aspects. To explore the tension between these two domains theoretically we must look at instances of that society in India which sustains on its own resources and not dependent on state sponsorship. And we should not be complacent with those instances where the state penetrated successfully into the society. Simultaneously, we ought to have those instances where the designs of the state are rejected, resisted, and defeated by Indian society.

Thus, these two contrasting paradigms would throw better light on our understanding of the tension that underlies the nationalist programme. In fact, this contrast—unlike in Chatterjee, where Mahatma Gandhi is interpreted as contributing to the nationalist programme—should help in locating the tension between the Indian state and its society. Partha Chatterjee in his work (1986) fails to bring out this configuration between Swami Vivekananda and Mahatma Gandhi, and underplays Gandhi's critique of modernity and overemphasizes the view where Gandhi promotes the modernist agenda of manoeuvring the emergence of an Indian state. In fact, Gandhi's critique of the Indian state remains very powerful. This ground can become an interesting platform to have larger debates, which have contemporary significance. Having elucidated on one important debate available in and for contemporary Indian philosophy, let me in the next chapter highlight yet another debate— this time between Savarkar and Gandhi—on yet another important theme concerning contemporary Indian society, namely, the relation between religion and politics.

NOTES

1. Gandhi was unable to meet Swami Vivekananda. He says, in his *Autobiography*,

   > Having seen enough of Brahmo Samaj, it was impossible to be satisfied without seeing Swami Vivekananda. So with great enthusiasm I went to Belur Math, mostly, or maybe all the way, on foot. I loved the sequestered site of the Math. I was disappointed and sorry to be told that the Swami was in his Calcutta house, lying ill, and could not be seen. (1976: 178)

2. Here it is important to note that though Vivekananda moved away from his earlier fascination for the modern West, however, from this he moved towards spiritualism and away from politics. While there seems to be some convergence between Vivekananda and Gandhi, with regard to the disenchantment with the modern West, there is no such convergence with

regard to what he moved into. That is, like Gandhi he did not turn towards the pre-modern realities and operate at the realm of politics too. This remains a major difference between Vivekananda and Gandhi.

Yet another important difference between Vivekananda and Gandhi is that the former pleaded for manliness, Gandhi on the other hand centralized femininity.

3. There are passages in Vivekananda that reveal his critical attitude towards the Western notion of progress. For instance, he says,

> Machines are making things cheap, making for progress and evolution, but millions are crushed, that one may become rich; while one becomes rich, thousands at the same time become poorer and poorer, and whole masses of human beings are made slaves. (1994, Vol. II: 96)

While there are these exceptions within Vivekananda, it is Gandhi who makes a more forceful and consistent case against the modern notion of progress. Unlike Vivekananda he does not vacillate.

4. Contextual variance and complexity associated with Vivekananda and also Gandhi do give rise to a range of ambiguities that cannot be circumvented by setting their works in 'chronological order'. Dermot Killingley traced the problem of interpreting Vivekananda to the haphazard compilation of his works. He says:

> The dating of his works is not always satisfactory, and the order in which they are presented in the *Collected Works* is largely haphazard. Although some works are grouped together chronologically, many from the same period are included in separate volumes, while some from different periods are grouped together. The effect is to obscure the development of his ideas, and to permit a false impression that they were all already formed before he set out for the United States. By setting in chronological order those works that are already dated, and investigating the internal and external evidence for the dating of the rest, it should be possible to approach a more realistic assessment of the development of his thought. In dating his works, it is legitimate to compare them with those already dated, with the publications of others, and with datable conversations or correspondence with others, in an attempt to establish a relative chronological place for them. (1999: 156–7)

While this might solve some limited problems, this would not make it easy to have 'a realistic assessment of the development of his thought', as he is not an antiseptic thinker presenting controlled doctrinaire consistency. In this sense, the project of complete works of doctrinaire thinkers in important respects differ from these 'septic' thinkers. So our attitude and expectations from the complete works of these thinkers may have to be different. Here I am not condoning the gaps and mistakes referred to by Killingley.

5. The following observation further reinforces the popularity of Vivekananda. Raychaudhuri says: 'In Madras and Calcutta, excited young men insisted on drawing Swamiji's carriage when he first returned from the West—a response which suggests something other than legitimate pride at a fellow countryman's success abroad'. (1988: 10)

6. Javeed Alam, however, contests Vivekananda's pro-Islam stance, though not in comparison to Bankim. He sees in Vivekananda an anti-Islamic and pro-Hindu stance, which is similar to the ideology of Hindu right. He quotes Vivekananda as having said:

> When the Mohammedans first came to India, what a great number of Hindus were there, but mark now today they have dwindled down! Everyday they will become less and less till they totally disappear.

Javeed Alam comments that these words,

> ...echo RSS sentiments since the 1920s, and those of the VHP (the most militant wing of the Sangh Parivar) today. Imperceptibly, before the turn of the century, the displacement becomes complete: the British recede into the background and the Musalman-Mohammedans take over. Implicit in these constructions are complex relations of thought, culture and power. All that Savarkar, Golwalkar or Advani have to do is alter the context and terms of these constructions and one can have a tenable political philosophy of nationalism, wherein all power is vested in the Hindus. (1999: 109–10)

He, however, in the very next page inserts a clarification and says:

> The references above to the RSS and VHP call for clarification. It is not the purpose of this argument to suggest an identity between great thinkers like Bankim and Vivekananda and latter-day Hindu communalists. The horizons of earlier nationalist thinkers or reformers were very large and the canvas on which they wrote was truly complex. But within this canvas there are certain thoughts and categorizations of people and communities which do not fit in with their own horizon. What they write about the Muslims—and this is especially true of Vivekananda—is easily detachable without doing violence to the nature of their argument (1999: 110).

Here I have two disagreements with Javeed Alam. I do not think it is possible or even necessary to make this detachment. If Vivekananda made these statements they must be ascribed to him. The complexity of their canvas notwithstanding they must be held responsible for these statements. Second, Javeed Alam fails to pay attention to those statements by Vivekananda praising Islam and the Prophet.

Unlike Javeed Alam, we have Tapan Raychaudhuri who sees no traces of Hindu revivalism in Vivekananda. According to him, Hindu revivalism is 'at best peripheral and for the most part antagonistic to Vivekananda's concerns'. (1999: 1)

Away from these I see Vivekananda's position as complex, and deciphering its nature perhaps may have to take into consideration, the speaker's intention, purpose, the given context and the hearer.

7. It is interesting to note that while Indians like Vivekananda bemoan the fact that India is not strong like the West, Western scholars such as Spengler, Husserl, Heidegger, and Leo Strauss were worried about the crisis in the Western civilization. Strauss attributes the loss of faith in itself as the reason for the decline of the West. (1964)

8. Along with these we do come across in Vivekananda's writings other reasons for the degradation of Indian society. For instance, the separation between the Buddhists and the Brahmins, he holds, 'is the cause of the downfall of India. That is why India is populated by three hundred million of beggars, and that is why India has been the slave of conquerors for the last thousand years'. (Vol. I, 1994: 23)

9. Ashis Nandy pithily describes as well as notes the limitation in this pose when he says:

> Contemporary Indian attitudes to woman and womanhood, when they are less than creative, are often the obverse of the colonial theory of statecraft: that is they accept the hierarchy, of gender qualities and either try to make 'men out of Indians' or to equal the West—or, as sometimes happens, Muslims—in masculinity. That is why between Vivekananda's theory of masculine Hinduism and Kipling's theory of the martial races, there is such a beautiful fit. It is this fit which has induced some of the great social reformers and thinkers of India—Gandhi is the obvious example—to emphasize the feminine at the expense of the masculine and to move out of the dominant culture of politics, even at the risk of sounding mystical or romantic. (1995: 215–16)

10. There is a need to distinguish between the two kinds of poverty, one is voluntary while the other is imposed; asceticism represents the first and social conditions the second. There are two dominant spiritual views, one maintaining that beyond the material world there is the spiritual one which underlies the four states in Hindu philosophy, but equally dominant is another view which maintains that spiritualism is attained by denying and necessarily passing through matter. Here we are discussing poverty in the social sense.

11. Stating a similarity between Gandhi and William Morris, Patrick Brantlinger says,

> Morris apparently believed that India was so steeped in poverty and superstition, albeit as a result of British 'force and fraud,' that he could not imagine it achieving immediate home rule, as he did for Ireland. (1996: 473)

Further, Brantlinger says,

> The restoration and reform of village culture, based on guilds and handicrafts, were to be main themes for Gandhi throughout his career. For Gandhi as for Morris, 'industrialism is...a curse' entailing imperialism, class exploitation, and the destruction of local autonomy.' The solution to India's problems could not come from imitating the industrialized, imperialist West but rather from restoring what was sound in the traditions of India's 'seven hundred thousand villages'... Gandhi wanted independent India to become a democracy whose basic units were villages. The obvious place to begin, moreover, was to 'reinstate the ancient cottage industry of handspinning' while rejecting all foreign and factory-made cloth. (1996: 479–80)

12. The subsequent developments—the modernization the world over, growing instances of violence, increased state control, the Bhopal disaster, and the cause for the Narmada Bachao Andolan, the recent GATT Treaty— clearly substantiate Gandhi's apprehension about modern civilization.

13. Critiquing Habermas' notion of universality and contrasting it with Gandhi, Thomas Pantham says:

> Gandhi's 'One world' project based on love and morality is in striking contrast to Habermas's project of repairing and furthering modernity through Western or, rather, Westerncentric rationality. (1988: 188)

14. I have in my earlier work (1995) pointed out that the relation between modernity and tradition in the West follows the sequential order, whereas in India it is simultaneous.

15. Even E.M.S. Namboodripad recognizes the fact that Gandhi related himself with the masses. He says,

> The one point of departure between Gandhi on the one hand, and all other politicians of those days on the other, was that, unlike the latter, *Gandhi associated himself with the masses of the people, their lives, problems, sentiments and aspirations.* [Emphasis author's] (1981: 19)

Further, he says:

> There was not one section of the people whose problems he did not study, whose miserable conditions he did not bring out, for whose comfort and solace he did not plead with his audience. It was this that enabled him to attract the various sections of the poor and downtrodden masses. (1981: 36)

16. For more on this see, my essay, 'Objectivism, Relativism/Pluralism: Study of Communities and Communalism' (1995a).

17. For universal meeting another universal, see Tagore's *The Religion of Man*, 2002: 76–83.

18. In identifying the Indian state with the Swami paradigm, I am not endorsing the view that the Indian state is properly implementing the Swami paradigm. I do not intend to establish one-to-one correspondence between the two. Further, in juxtaposing the interface between Indian state and society, while recognizing the success of the Indian state and its oppressive activities on Indian society, we also have to be open to those instances where Indian society defeats the designs of the Indian state.

■

CHAPTER THREE

Savarkar and Gandhi
From Politicizing Religion to Spiritualizing Politics

Having highlighted the paradigmatic difference between two important contemporary Indian philosophers, Swami Vivekananda and Mahatma Gandhi, I shall in this chapter lay bare another important and fundamental debate regarding the relation between religion and politics. This is an important theme underlying contemporary Indian society, on which two important contemporary Indian philosophers, V.D. Savarkar and M.K. Gandhi have expressed radically different views.[1] This difference has eluded the attention of scholars. Moreover, there have been attempts to conflate and dissolve the difference between Gandhi and Hindutva thereby projecting a false commonality (Bilgrami 1994).[2] This conflation is not only incorrect but politically naïve and that is dangerous. For instance, this conflation, where Gandhi is pushed nearer to the ideology of Hindutva, has become a blessing in disguise for the ideologues of Hindutva and they have, in fact, received it wholeheartedly. They, in turn, further consolidated this similarity by selectively using specifically Gandhian vocabulary such as *swadeshi*, which continues to ignite the imagination of the Indian electorate, in the election manifesto of their political party, namely, Bharatiya Janata Party (BJP). All this has strengthened the political programme of Hindutva.

Apart from this, to forcefully counterpose the differences between Gandhi and Savarkar, I shall demolish the opposition posited between

Enlightenment[3] and Hindutva. I shall point out how the dangers of Hindutva have to be located not merely in its opposition to Enlightenment as argued by some like Sumit Sarkar (1993)[4] who posits the antagonism between Liberal-secular ideology of the Enlightenment and the ideology of Hindutva.[5] I shall instead point out the incorporation of Enlightenment ideals and elements within the Hindutva fold.[6] This attempted proximity of some of the important aspects of Enlightenment by the Hindutva, further reinforces the opposition between Savarkar and Gandhi. Highlighting this proximity is important as critics have generally assumed that just as Gandhi is critical of the Enlightenment and is for the pre-modern so too is Savarkar.

To facilitate a forceful critique of Hindutva, a term often used though its semantic structure is not clearly noted, it is necessary to clarify its contents.[7] Moreover, to embark on a forceful critique of Hindutva, it is necessary to release it from the grips of those who implicate it with wrong or mistaken associations. I shall then repudiate those attempts that conflate Gandhi with Hindutva.[8]

In the first formulation, Sarkar wrongly characterizes Hindutva as merely religious and traditional while contrasting it with the Enlightenment discourse. In contrast to Sarkar's punctuation of Hindutva as religious, an attempt is made here to point out that the ideology of Hindutva did incorporate within its fold important modern elements. In fact, V.D. Savarkar, the ideologue of Hindutva, emphasized the urgency to develop modern Western science, its technology, industry, and knowledge systems in India, to be used for both achieving material prosperity and to '*militarise Hindudom*'. Alongside, this ideology incorporated within its fold the modern obsession with political unity and cultural homogeneity, and a veritable rejection of cultural differences and pluralism.

These are important aspects of modernity having their origin in the Enlightenment discourse and they attracted Savarkar. This being so, it becomes necessary to re-examine the elements of modernity incorporated in the ideology of Hindutva and in this context reassess the characterization of Hindutva as religious or traditional.[9]

I

In contrast to Sumit Sarkar's description of Hindutva as religious, I shall in the following pages argue that Hindutva is a modified modern phenomenon which, far from representing religious aspects, has in fact adopted a number of important elements of the Enlightenment such as its obsession with unity, fascination for science and technology, and instrumental rationality. It is therefore necessary to re-examine the elements of modernity incorporated in the ideology of Hindutva, and in this context, reassess the characterization of Hindutva as religious or traditional.

In alluding to the similarities and overlaps between the Enlightenment and Hindutva, it is not suggested that the former leads to the latter; it only puts forth the suggestion that it might not be so feasible for the Enlightenment to be used as a weapon to attack Hindutva, particularly for homogenizing plural Indian society. There is yet another limitation surrounding Enlightenment, given its commitment to the ontological priority of individualism. It is hostile to cultural pluralism. Another well-known historian, Romila Thapar, in her essay entitled, 'Syndicated Moksa', also criticizes Hindutva for homogenizing the plural Hindu society. The precariousness in this kind of a stance is caused by the hostility exhibited by the Enlightenment and its branches, Liberalism and Marxism. I shall return to this later while discussing Crowder's view on the relation between Liberalism and pluralism. What becomes clear, therefore, is that it might be safer to critique Hindutva from another point of view, such as Gandhi's.

ENLIGHTENMENT AND HINDUTVA

Hindutva, says Sarkar, is religious, traditional and that, 'by its very definition [it] has to preach total adherence and defence towards Hindu tradition' (1993: 166). In addition, he offers a cluster of arguments in contrasting Liberal-secular ideology, which is part of the Enlightenment discourse, from the ideology of Hindutva. They are:

(i) He sharply contrasts fascism with the Enlightenment. In support of this contrast, he recalls Giovanni Gentile who defined fascism as a 'revolt against positivism' or Mussolini who in 1933 had condemned the 'movement of the 18th century visionaries and Encyclopaedists' along with 'teleological conceptions of progress'. Sarkar, in this context, also recalls another peroration of the Italian dictator, in July 1934, where he called for an end to an 'intellectualising and of those sterile intellectuals who are a threat to the nation'. Last, Sarkar reminds us that Hitler at the Nuremberg Nazi Congress in 1935 similarly exalted that 'heart', the 'faith', the 'inner voice' of the German '*volk* over hair-splitting intelligence' (Sarkar 1993: 165). In this way, Sarkar conclusively establishes the antagonism between Enlightenment and fascism.

Having established this antagonism, he goes on to show how the fascist ideology in Europe that had combined with the already quite widespread elements viz., crudely nationalist, racist, and, in Germany, anti-Semitic prejudices with fragments from much more sophisticated philosophies, in fact, owed something to a general turn-of-the-century's move away from what were felt to be the sterile rigidities of Enlightenment rationalism. This moving away from the Enlightenment rationalism, that is related to the rise of the fascist ideology, says Sarkar, has relevance today, as not dissimilar ideas have become current intellectual coin in the West, and by extension they have started to influence the Indian academic life. (1993: 164–5)

(ii) Further, Sarkar characterizes Hindutva as fascist. He rightly notes two chilling similarities between Hindutva and fascism. They are: (a) 'The Muslim [in Hindutva] becomes the near equivalent of the Jew' (1993: 165); and, (b) 'The Sangh Parivar, similarly [like Nazi fascism] tries to establish its claim to be truly and uniquely "national" by a democratic argument. Hindu interests should prevail always in India...' (1993: 165). He, however, finds fault with their democratic argument, as 'democracy logically must connote two other features in addition to the rule of majority: protection of rights of minority ways of life and opinions, and, even more crucially, the legal possibility that the political minority of today can win electoral majority in the future and thus peacefully change the government' (1993: 165).

(iii) Having distinguished the Enlightenment from both fascism and Hindutva, he goes on to show the affinity between the critique of the Enlightenment or Postmodernism and the ideology of Hindutva (and fascism). He observes that many of the ideologists of the Sangh Parivar are largely unaware of the varied possibilities of Postmodernism. But academic fashions, such as Said's 'Orientalism' with its critique of colonial discourse, can reduce the resistance of intellectuals to the idea of Hindutva. He maintains that Said's *Orientalism*, for instance, has given rise to forms of indigenization not very easily distinguishable from the standard Sangh Parivar argument. Here, according to Sarkar, the Sangh Parivar's argument as evident in Savarkar is that '...Hindutva is superior to Islam and Christianity (and by extension, to creations of the modern West like science, democracy or Marxism) because of its allegedly unique indigenous roots'. (1993: 165)

(iv) Finally, though Sarkar in the beginning characterized Hindutva as traditional, or religious, he acknowledges the fact that Hindutva does effect transformations and in the process homogenizes the cultural pluralism of Hindus. Sarkar does not see this to be part of the Enlightenment. In fact, he seems to perceive the Enlightenment as pro-pluralism, whereas its basic tenets stand for plural individual interests. The basic tenets of the Enlightenment do not nurture pluralism, rather they positively erode them. Moreover, Sarkar makes the charge that Hindutva is

...really homogenising and changing Hindu beliefs and practices on a truly colossal scale... But the vast and enormously variegated Hindu world has never had what the VHP is trying to make out of Ram and Ayodhya—a single, supreme deity and pilgrimage centre, steamrolling out of existence differences of region, sect, caste, gender, class.... (1993: 166).

Here, Sarkar is indeed critical of Hindutva's homogenizing of plural Hindu beliefs and practices.

The summary of the cluster of arguments advanced by Sarkar can be stated as follows: (i) fascism is antagonistic to Enlightenment; (ii) Hindutva is fascist; (iii) a critique of the Enlightenment ideals by Postmodernism is closer to both fascism and Hindutva; and, (iv) Hindutva homogenizes the pluralistic Hinduism or Hindu. In making this last point, namely, (iv), Sarkar in fact has deviated from his other observations on Hindutva made in (i) and (iii).

I readily accept (i) and (ii). However, I contest (iii). In fact, my terms of contesting (iii) partly use Sarkar's own arguments, namely, (iv). I begin with (iv). I concur with Sarkar's attribution of homogeneity to Hindutva. However, if Sarkar is objecting to Hindutva's project of homogenizing plural Hindu beliefs and practices, then finding a similar objection in the Enlightenment discourse will be difficult because the Enlightenment, which is committed to individualism either as an ontological category (for instance, 'man-in-the-state-of-nature' in Social Contract philosophies) or a political category (in other schools such as Liberalism) endorses homogeneity and is hostile to pluralism.

ENLIGHTENMENT, HOMOGENEITY, AND PLURALISM

The Enlightenment's stand towards homogeneity and pluralism needs to be deciphered. Immediately we can point out that Enlightenment rationality is 'instrumental reason'—used by Social Contract philosophers and later executed in modern science and technology—and it cannot accept pluralism. Each of these plural communities has what Akeel Bilgrami calls 'internal reason'. The reason that is advocated by the Enlightenment thinkers (with exceptions like in Hegel) is not 'internal reason' but 'instrumental reason'. Instrumental reason per se rejects pluralism, which thrives on cultural differences.[10]

Moreover, within the Social Contract theory, there is no place envisaged for pluralism. Its overriding normativity is bereft of the description of plural social institutions. In fact, all three Social Contract philosophers—Hobbes, Rousseau, and Locke—have rejected natural communities and 'intermediary natural social institutions'. Commenting on the idea of state and power in Hobbes, Ebenstein says:

Hobbes is vehemently opposed to division of powers or mixed government...[and] to keep the authority of the state strong, Hobbes advises the sovereign not to allow the growth of groups and institutions that intervene between state and individual. (1972: 361)

That is, Hobbes not only rejected the division of political power but also rejected anything mediating between the state and the individual. Making a general observation on the modern theories of state, MacIver (1970) observes that in the making of modern society,

...it has usually been the state...which has sought to prevent further differentiation by making all other organizations a part of its own structure and subject to the conformity it imposed. Hobbes...had denounced free associations as being like 'worms in the entrails of the natural man', and as late as the end of the eighteenth [century] the French Revolution had sought in the name of liberty to abolish all corporate bodies. Rousseau no less than Burke, the philosopher of revolution as much as the philosopher of reaction...still believed in the 'universal partnership' or the 'total surrender' which made the membership of a society culturally inclusive. (1970: 117)

Here it is necessary to clarify that though the society and the general will in the Social Contract theories are formed by individuals, the general will here is not empirical but a rational concept, the latter dominating the former. For instance, Rousseau in the *Social Contract* says that:

Of itself the people wills always the good, but of itself it by no means always sees it. The general will is always in the right, but the judgement which guides it is not always enlightened. It must be got to see object as they are, and sometimes as they ought to appear to it... (Rousseau 1952: 31)

Thus, the notion of rationalism in the political philosophy of Social Contract philosophers is not empirical and without empiricism in politics, democracy is not possible. Therefore, the rationalism of the Enlightenment as embodied in Social Contract philosophers is against pluralism and it positively endorses homogeneity. Given the primacy of their normativity, there is hardly any place for the empirical choices of the individual. Even when they do talk about democracy, like in Locke, their democracy eventually subscribes to majoritarianism. In fact, Social Contract theories have completely discarded the plural social institutions. They have proposed beginning all over again with atomized homogenized individuals in the state-of-nature. They have rejected institutions as given and accepted only those institutions which are man-made. They cannot possibly, therefore, be said to have accepted pluralism. Paradoxically, the limitation of democracy Sarkar attributes to fascism and Hindutva, exemplified by the secondary position given to Jews and Muslims respectively, is also true of Locke, the most flexible Social Contract philosopher.

Thus, we can conclude that Social Contract theories are indeed intolerant towards pluralism and difference. In fact, it is evident from the above discussion that these philosophers bolstered political unity. Their obsession with political unity is necessarily related to their hostility towards cultural difference. This provides the basis and context for the communitarians and multiculturalists' critique of liberalism. So, Social Contract philosophies, which are a part of the Enlightenment, too are committed to homogenizing plural cultures. Given the adherence of Social Contract philosophers to the ontological priority of individualism (formulated as 'man-in-the-state-of-nature') and their rejection of any social institution as given, and their acceptance of any social institutions as man-made, they cannot possibly be said to accept pluralism. This hostility towards pluralism continues to prevail even in the later Enlightenment schools such as the Liberal Utilitarians.

In the writings of Liberals such as Jeremy Bentham and J.S. Mill, the obsession with unity is considerably toned down. However, the fact remains that Liberals, given their normative project of individualism and liberty, do not positively promote community difference. In fact, the difference that the Liberals concede and even bolster is different individual preferences, and not community difference, whereas what pluralism is seeking is the community difference. It is in this context that, George Crowder (1994) in debate with Isaiah Berlin and Bernard Williams (1994) raises the question regarding the relation between Liberalism and pluralism. For him, not:

...only does pluralism provide no support for liberalism, it positively undermines the liberal case, since it is always open to the pluralist to ask, why not the illiberal option? A question arises whether pluralism, far from implying liberalism, is even compatible with the reasoned justification of liberal norms (1994: 304).

The overriding normativity of Liberalism, which includes individualism and liberty, is incompatible with the cultural aspects crucial to pluralism. It is this fundamental feature of Liberalism that made Anschutz way back in 1963 to distinguish the utilitarianism of David Hume from Bentham and J.S. Mill. In Anschutz's interpretation, for Hume the principle of utility is a description of received morality, it is the principle for interpreting the existing morality. In contrast, for Bentham, says Anschutz, 'the principle of utility [is] not...one that we ordinarily do obey but simply one that we ought to obey' (1963: 11). Further, the 'anthropological and sociological' concern in Hume is what made A.C. MacIntyre distinguish him from the utilitarianism of Mill. He says:

The difference between Mill's utilitarianism and Hume's lies in this: that if we take some such statement as 'We ought to do whatever is to the advantage of most people', this for Mill would be a moral principle which it would be morally wrong to deny, but which it would make sense to deny. Whereas for Hume to deny this statement would be senseless, for it would detach 'ought' from the notion of a consensus of interest and so evacuate it of meaning. Roughly speaking, for Mill such a principle would be a contingent moral truth; for Hume it would be a necessary truth underlying morality. (1969: 41)

Therefore, Hume's utilitarian principle, which is the principle for interpreting the existing morality, is marginalized and the utilitarianism of Bentham and Mill becomes central. However, Hume's utilitarianism is closer to pluralism and not the utilitarianism of Bentham–Mill.

Contemporary Liberal thinkers like John Rawls, Joseph Raz, and Will Kymlicka, says Bhikhu Parekh, have made 'considerable advance over that of their classical predecessors and opened up lines of inquiry', with regard to pluralism. While conceding this, he however, says that this is 'inadequate' for the following reasons:

[i] Take their account of autonomy. As they understand it, culture helps individuals develop their capacity for autonomy, which then transcends it and views it and the wider world untainted by its provenance. This is a misleading account of the relation between the two...[ii] directly, or indirectly, and subtly or crudely, liberals continue to absolutize liberalism...[iii] in their discussion of

how to treat the so-called nonliberals' ways of life, liberal writers adopt one of two strategies...confront nonliberal with a full blooded liberal vision and attack them for failing to measure up to it. (Barry, 1991)... Others may...thin down liberal principles to what they take to be their minimum content, and make tolerance of nonliberal cultures conditional upon their acceptance of it. (Bhikhu Parekh 2000: 110–11)

All this exposes liberalism's hostile attitude towards pluralism. This Enlightenment obsession with unity did not merely remain at the theoretical level. It, in fact, formed the theoretical basis for the transformation of plural Western societies into nation-states.[11] In this context, let us discuss the project of nationalism, which is based on the theoretical assumptions of the Enlightenment idea of man and state. Ernest Gellner, in his work (1983) has discussed some key features of nationalism.

Nationalism is an enabling agent for the realization of the 'universal urge for liberty and progress'. However, nationalism is not offered as an alternative political ideal to Western society but is thrust upon it as a necessity. This necessity demands transformation of the plural societies against the self-image of the idea of nationalism. Further, Gellner justifies this transformation by invoking the distinction between the 'wild' and 'high' cultures. The 'wild' here refers to the traditional agrarian societies preceding nationalism. These societies, admits Gellner, are like the savage plants that produce and reproduce 'spontaneously' without a 'conscious design', surviving in a 'nature given atmosphere'. The 'high cultures' on the other hand, represent nations, which 'possess a complexity and richness, most usually sustained by literacy and by specialized personnel...' have to be nurtured 'in a new, specially blended and artificially sustained air or medium' (Gellner 1983: 50-1). These mediums are created and maintained by the state, on whom the people of the nation are made to depend. Contrasting this new dependency on the state necessitated by the 'high' culture with the agrarian societies, Gellner says that the man of the 'wild' culture, unlike the man of the 'high' culture, is not solely dependent on the state for support. To quote Gellner, 'In the agrarian age it [society] sometimes has this [political support and underpinning] and benefited from it, but at other times it could dispense with political protection and that was indeed one of its strengths'. (1983: 51)

The transformation referred to above is not smooth, and it is not governed by sympathy or understanding of what is being transformed. The transformation, admits Gellner, is not an awakening of an old, latent, dominant force but, 'a period of turbulent readjustment, in which either political boundaries, or cultural ones, or both, were being modified, so as to satisfy the nationalist imperatives...and this period of transition was...violent and conflict-ridden...' (1983: 40).

In this sense, even the project of nationalism tends to emphasize the primacy of individualism, demands the need for the individuals to disown or not to evoke their community considerations. All these make many aspects of the Enlightenment not favourable to pluralism. In contrast, they tend to homogenize individuals.[12] So Sarkar's strategy of critiquing Hindutva for homogenizing plural societies as a counter point to the Enlightenment though well-intended is inappropriate. Having discussed the Enlightenment's hostility towards pluralism, let me now turn to elucidate those aspects of the Enlightenment which Hindutva sought to incorporate into its fold. In the above I have presented an elaborate discussion of the Enlightenment as I find quite often in the case of Indian social scientists a narrow and propagandistic version of the Enlightenment.

To come back to Savarkar after clearing him from Sarkar's allegations, Savarkar, unlike what is attributed to him, does not reject modern science, and in fact, praised it. According to Dhananjay Keer, Savarkar, '...appeal[ed] to the nation that it is the duty of every thinking man to promote the principles of science in every department of life. Without it, no nation can hope to survive the present stage...' (Keer 1966: 205). In his article, 'Machine: Boon or Curse' (2003: 503–7) he asserted that:

Machine has made it possible for man[to] stay beneath water, rise high up in the sky. Machine has made man far-reaching, far-seeing, far-speaking and far-hearing. Machine has conferred upon man blessings which no prophets could give or no penance could secure. Mankind owes its present civilization entirely to the use of machine and thus far from being a curse, is a wonderful boon which has bestowed supernatural powers upon this human race! (Savarkar in *Savarkar Samagra*, Vol. 7, p. 506, translated by Keer in his *Veer Savarkar*, 1966: 205)

This in a way explains right-wing's leaning towards modern technology epitomized in the Pokhran nuclear testing, and its consistent pro-nuclear policy. To this we can add instances where Savarkar is critical of the Hindu tradition, particularly its superstitions. He often contrasts traditional superstition with scientific rationalism and favours the latter. In the context of explaining the Lisbon earthquake in eighteenth century, he, in his article, entitled, 'Decrease in Fear of God Will Increase Technological Progress', (*Savarkar Samagra*, Vol. 7, 2003: 497–8), says that, 'It was quite all right when we did not know the causes of such things [earthquakes], but to stick to these superstitions even when science has revealed the causes of such calamities is simply absurd' (as translated by Keer 1966: 204). Further, in his essay, 'Story of Nane Phadnavis', (*Savarkar Samagra*, Vol. 7, 2003: 498–500) he writes: 'What actually matters is scientific accuracy and not astrological superstition. Astrology cannot save what science has doomed and where safety is assured by science, astrology cannot endanger it' (as translated by Keer 1966: 205). In yet another essay entitled, 'Machine', (*Savarkar Samagra*, Vol. 7, 2003: 496–7) he complained that, 'We have allowed the Britishers to crush everything that was with us, but not that precious possession of ours, our credulous superstitions!' (as translated by Keer 1966: 204).

Further, almost sounding orientalist, Savarkar compliments the West on its material progress and admits the backwardness of Indians. In his letter to his brother from the Andaman, Savarkar writes that:

The Americans need Vedanta philosophy and so does England, for they have developed their life to that fullness, richness and manliness—to Kshatriyahood and so stand on the threshold of that Brahminhood, wherein alone the capacity to read and realize such philosophy can co-exist. But India is not. We are at present all Shudras and can't claim access to the *Vedas* and Vedanta... We, as a nation, are unfit for these sublime thoughts... Let us study history, political science, science, economy; live worthily in this world, fulfil the householders' duties and then the philosophic dawn might come. ('Machine' in *Savarkar Samagra*, Vol. 7, 2003 as translated by Keer 1966: 137)

Thus, contrary to what Sarkar asserts while characterizing Savarkar as an advocate of the superiority of Hindus and as someone who rejected modern science, we do come across instances where Savarkar admits the religious superstitions in Hinduism, and the material backwardness of the Hindus, and celebrates the West's success in its modern science. Since Hindutva attempts to incorporate some aspects of the Enlightenment, which provide overlapping space, Enlightenment cannot possibly be a right framework to critique Hindutva.[13]

Keer, Savarkar's biographer, reports that Savarkar acknowledged the strength of Europe and commented: 'In Europe people belong mostly to one religion. There the strife between races aimed at predominance and domination. In India it is a question of rival religions, where kidnapping and conversion are ostensibly done in the name of religion to strengthen a rival faith' (Keer 1966: 139). Savarkar envisages his programme for Hindus along Western lines.

To recall, the West, particularly the modern West, irresistibly fascinates Savarkar. There are two streams in him with regard to Hindu society. One, in comparison to the West, he admits that Hindu society is not strong. Two, he accepts the strength of the Hindu society. Savarkar shuttles between these two opposite views. This makes his position towards Hindu society very ambivalent. (This ambivalence inherent in the Indian nationalism of the Indian National Congress is well discussed by Chatterjee in his 1986 work.)

From the above discussion, we can infer that Savarkar is not advocating an indigenous world view but endorsing modernity. Further, unlike others who use the word 'motherland' to designate India, Savarkar uses the term 'fatherland' indicating the changed nature of his politics. He says that this 'land to him [Hindu] is not only a Pitribhu but a Punyabhu, not only a fatherland but a holyland' (1989: 111).

I think if we keep this broad framework in mind, we can read the politics of the right wing in India better. It is interesting that the BJP has inherited this general framework of Savarkar, thus there is continuity between Savarkar and the BJP. The BJP too, like Savarkar, is pro-modern, in the sense that it too seeks to do a West on India. For instance, BJP has supported the idea of modernizing Indian society, this notwithstanding its *swadeshi* card. This becomes evident when we examine its response to huge modern projects such as the Narmada Valley Dam, or the Dabol project. It is in this context that we have to locate the contemporary aspiration or hope of some and fear for many, that the BJP will implement the globalization projects in India faster than the Congress. However, the BJP like Savarkar continues to display an ambivalent attitude towards pre-modern Indian society. Let me now make an independent critique of Savarkar by showing the violent politics that his ideology inaugurated in seeking to transform Hinduism into Hindutva.

POLITICIZING RELIGION BY MILITARIZING HINDUISM: V.D. SAVARKAR

Keeping these broad similarities between the Enlightenment and Hindutva or the latter's incorporation of the former in mind, let us analyse how Savarkar develops his theory of political unity as embodied in Hindutva, by transforming Hinduism. Distinguishing Hinduism from Hindutva Savarkar says:

It [Hinduism]...means the school or system of religions the Hindus follow...'Hindutva' is far more comprehensive and refers not only to the religious aspect of the Hindu people as the word 'Hinduism' does but comprehends even their cultural, linguistic, social and political aspects as well. It is more or less akin to 'Hindu Polity' and its nearly exact translation would be 'Hinduness'. The...word 'Hindudom' means the Hindu people spoken of collectively. It is a collective name for the Hindu world, just as Islam denotes the Moslem world or Christiandom denotes the Christian world. (1984: 78)

The most important idea that lurks behind Savarkar's political views is the slogan that he often repeats, namely: *Hinduize all politics and militarize Hindudom.*[14] (Savarkar 1967: 1)

Let me elaborate the various aspects of such a recommendation. For Savarkar, Hindu philosophy is not to be considered as a mere religious order confining itself to spiritual and ritualistic activities. He condemns the ritualistic aspect of the Hindu religion that is Hinduism. In this context, he distinguishes Hinduism from Hindutva. A Hindu need not necessarily accept the authority of the Vedas, as 'a man can be as truly a Hindu as any without believing even in the Vedas as an independent religious authority...' (1989: 81). Hinduism that is usually identified with Vedanta philosophy is not central to the Hindu; rather, to Savarkar it is only a 'derivative, a fraction, a part of Hindutva' (1989: 2). To him, the '...concept of Hindutva is an idea embodying...principle of unity.' It is '...not [just] a word but a history. Not only the spiritual or religious history of our people as at times it is mistaken to be by being confounded with the other cognate term Hinduism, but a history in full' (1989: 3); consisting of one language (Hindi); one name (Hindu); a common culture and law; all are pre-British and pre-Islamic to him (1989: 71). Hindu is one for whom the S/Hindusthan is not only a fatherland but also a holy land. (1989: 113)

Such an opening could remain a mere theoretical formulation. So, he provides flesh to this by his second statement namely, *militarizing Hinduism.* Before discussing the nature of militarism, let me clarify that to Savarkar militarism is not something alien to Hindus, as he says, '...the martial spirit in the Hindu Race...lay dormant and suppressed for want of opportunity and encouragement' (1967: 4). Further, he says, 'The children of Konkan, as it is said regarding the children of Britain, begin to play with the waves as soon as they begin to play with toys and have an inborn aptitude to make the best fighting material for the sea forces of our nation' (1967:44). This inborn militancy is historically validated by Savarkar when he says that it is these Hindu castes like the Bhandaris and Kharvis, that once rendered the Maratha navy a terror over the Portuguese and the English and had inflicted several crushing defeats in naval engagements on them, as for example, when in a sea-fight the wellknown English warship *Revenge* was captured by the Marathas (1967: 44).

And,

...it is Vikramaditya, 'the shaka-ri', the 'Huna-ri', the Great Hindu warrior King who defeated, demolished and drove the Shakas and Huns—the alien non-Hindu invaders and liberated our Bharat-varsha. '[15] (1967: 106)

Therefore, Hindus are naturally disposed towards militarism. This, Savarkar claims, is also historically demonstrated. Then, what accounts for their passive existence? According to him, the British government deliberately suppressed the naval instincts till date (1967: 44). It is this suppression of martial elements in Hindus that made British colonialism in India possible. Savarkar, while admitting the military superiority of the British, recommends to Indians the path followed by their colonial rulers. Given the context of colonial oppression, the British did not allow their subjects to inculcate militarism. In a way, this may be the precondition for their survival. It is in this context, says Savarkar, that the 'war has actually begun to batter at our doors,' that is, at the doors of Hindus. The British government for its own survival has 'thrown open, under pressure of circumstances, the services in the navy to the Hindus...' (1967: 44).

Joining the British army would help the British. However, joining the army has the following advantage for the Indians: (a) then and then alone they (Hindus) will be in a position to defend their hearths and homes from the ravages of the war and to suppress any internal anti-Hindu anarchy; (b) moreover the martial mentality and capacity thus developed today by the Hindus are bound to prove an incalculable asset to the national strength even after the war (1967: 42). While the participation by the Hindus in the war might help the British only during the war, there is a long-term gain for the Hindus themselves in the form of militarizing the Hindu race. Once the Hindu race is militarized, the British might naturally leave India or they may be driven out. Therefore, to Savarkar, the strategy should be to get into the enemy's camp and subvert the designs of the enemy from within.

To Savarkar, '...Hindus shall never be able to defend...[them]selves effectively unless...[they] get military-minded and get trained into an up-to-date warfare' (1967: 45). Hence, the need to militarize the Hindu race and get it trained up to an up-to-date military efficiency. And '...secure permanently a dominant position for the Hindus in the Indian army, navy and air-force...' (1967: 5). To accomplish this more effectively, he advocates the need to '...liberalise the social outlook of the Hindu race, get rid materially of present economic unemployment, give a fillip to industrialization, render the Hindu military-minded, spirited and valorous and secure and stabilise the Hindu strength in Indian Military Forces of all arms' (1967: 6). He is jubilant about the fact that thousands '...are being trained...in ordnance factories, shipyards and in several other war-crafts'. (1967: 4)

All these transformations and changes would make the unity of India possible. It is from this obsession with unity that Savarkar looks at Muslims in India. He says that no state,

...in the world can allow that section which openly aims to create 'a state within a state,' to dominate it. Any Hindu state which commits this suicidal error of delivering its military or police or legislature or such other vital factors over to the Moslem majority cannot but be doomed to destruction. The same holds good as regards the Indian state. (1967: 72)

The place that Savarkar envisages for the Muslims is: 'Hindus are prepared to guarantee legitimate safeguards to minorities but can never tolerate their efforts to create a state within a state as the League of Nations puts it' (1967: 40). In another context, he says that if the Muslim minority is really afraid of the Hindu majority then 'the only effective way to save themselves is to befriend the majority, to owe undivided love and loyalty to our common motherland and to the centralised Indian State' (1967: 164), thereby demanding that the religious Hindu safeguard the political unity of India.

Savarkar's notion of political unity has two important components, namely, obsession with unity and positive rejection of difference and dissent. As already noted, this idea of political unity closely resembles the notion of the state in the Social Contract philosophies. These schools have bolstered the unity of the state. This is very much evident in Hobbes and Rousseau. In both these thinkers there is no place envisaged for cultural difference. While Locke allows the possibility of dissent by the minority, he too finally resorts to the wisdom of the majority. The minorities in Locke are no different from the Muslim minority in Savarkar's framework and Jews in fascism. Both Muslims in Hindutva and Jews in fascism are similar to the minorities in Locke who finally have to obey the dictates of the majority. (The difference between minoritism in fascism and minoritism in Locke is that the former is racist and the latter rationalistic.) Of course, there is no minority allowed in Hobbes and Rousseau. In this Hindutva seeks to inhabit the philosophical foundations of the Enlightenment. This underlying similarity needs to be more pointedly focused than the deceptive differences pointed out by Sarkar. Thus, contrary to Sarkar, who formulates the relation between the Enlightenment on the one hand, and fascism, and Hindutva on the other as antagonistic, it is necessary to highlight Savarkar's attempt to incorporate aspects of modernity within Hindutva. Here we can say that the passage from Hinduism to Hindutva is a journey where religious elements are rejected, or radically transformed into the masculinized politics of modernity by injecting into them political elements—militancy, power, a closed unity and so on. Thus, the Hindutva ideology is not merely religious or an expression of tradition, but a new phenomenon. It does refer to religious symbols but not without radically transforming these symbols and making them agents of politics. Instead of merely equating Hindutva as religious or traditional, we must closely scrutinize the contents of religion in Hindutva. In other words, the politics of Hindutva needs to be exposed not merely because it is too traditional but also because it is too modern. The violent Rama that came to represent the Masjid-Mandir controversy is an instance in this context. It is necessary to take serious note of the modificatory nature of Hindutva from Hinduism. It is this proximity between modernity and Hindutva that is mostly neglected in the recent discussions on communalism.[16] In discussions within the Liberal-secularist discourse, the ideology of Hindutva comes to be portrayed as traditional, religious, etc. The mere fact that Hindutva employs religious terms and symbols should not make us conclude, as it often has, that it is backward-looking and traditional. However, Ashis Nandy highlighted this proximity between modernity and Hindutva and also the antagonism between Hinduism and Hindutva. While contrasting Mahatma Gandhi with both Hindu orthodoxy and British colonialists, he wrote:

...[Gandhi] rejected the British as well as the Brahmanic-Kshatriya equation between manhood and dominance, between masculinity and legitimate violence, and between femininity and passive submissiveness. (1989: 74)

Further, he says that, 'Hinduism and Hindutva now stand face to face, not yet ready to confront each other, but aware that the confrontation will have to come some day...' Speaking pessimistically, he says, 'Hindutva will be the end of Hinduism'. (1991)

Instead of merely regarding Hindutva as religious, following the insight of Nandy, we must closely scrutinize the contents of religion in Hindutva. Thus, the opposition between the Enlightenment and Hindutva cannot be taken for granted. In pointing out these common sources, it is not my intention to club the Enlightenment with the ideology of Hindutva, but point out those aspects the latter has taken from the former. Here I am only suggesting that in our discussion of Liberalism and Hindutva ideology, the Indian Liberals have to consciously negotiate these similarities and common agendas (their hostility towards difference and pluralism, their attitude towards modern science and technology, their views on globalization, and so on). Merely evoking a positive reading of the Enlightenment philosophy to expose the politics of Hindutva is not only insufficient but can be counter-productive. This demolishes the opposition posited between the Enlightenment and Hindutva, and facilitates a better and more forceful contrast between Savarkar and Gandhi, and shows how Gandhi is diametrically opposed, in some important respects, to Savarkar.[17]

II

SPIRITUALIZING POLITICS: GANDHI

Having contested the antagonism between Liberalism and Hindutva, I now contest Akeel Bilgrami's view wherein Gandhi[18] is alleged to be encouraging the communal Hindu elements in the national movement, thus relapsing into the Hindu right. Bilgrami, while conceding the humanism inherent in Gandhi's politics, however, alleges that,

...it is foolish and sentimental to deny the Brahmanical elements in it [i.e., in Gandhi's politics]. There is the well-known fact that Gandhi, no less than the Chitpavan nationalist Tilak (however different their nationalist sensibilities were in other respects), encouraged the communal Hindu elements in the national movement by using Hindu symbolism to mobilize mass nationalist feeling. (1994: 1751)

Thus, Bilgrami eventually knocks down the Gandhian politics together with the Hindutva ideology. Gandhi, however, I would like to maintain, seeks to repudiate the two dominant political realities of contemporary India, namely, the ideology of Hindutva as well as modernity. Nandy remarks:

Perhaps Hindutva too will die a natural death. But then, many things that die in colder climes in the course of a single winter survive in the tropics for years. Maybe the death of Hindutva will not be as natural as that of some other ideologies. Maybe, post-Gandhian Hinduism will have to take advantage of the democratic process to help Hindutva to die a slightly unnatural death. Perhaps that euthanasia will be called politics. (*Times of India*, 18 February 1991)

Here I also recall the hope as recorded by Madan when he says:

Perhaps men of religion such as Mahatma Gandhi would be our best teachers on the proper relation between religion and politics—values and interests—understanding not only the possibilities of interreligious understanding, which is not the same as an emaciated notion of mutual tolerance or respect, but also opening out avenues of a spiritually justified limitation of the role of religious institutions and symbols in certain areas of contemporary life. (1999: 408)

In direct opposition to Savarkar, Gandhi urges spiritualizing political life and institutions. He would find in Savarkar's Hindutva, as in the modern civilization, an absence of religious elements. In stark contrast to Savarkar, Gandhi is pleading for transferring the spiritual elements into the political domain in order to transform it.[19]

Before discussing the real differences between Gandhi and Savarkar, let me note some similarities shared by both. For instance, both rejected the separation of religion and politics. Savarkar writes, 'The Hindus never looked upon religion as a means of worldly strength and social solidarity. This is in my opinion their fundamental blunder from the point of view of natural strength and solidarity' (in Keer 1966: 142).

Moreover, for Gandhi, 'Politics cannot be divorced from religion. Politics divorced from religion becomes debasing' (1986: 374); a death trap because it kills the soul; it is like a corpse fit only for burning (1950: 14). 'Modern culture and modern civilization' are the examples of 'such politics' (1986: 374). Politics, to Gandhi, is as essential as religion, the former subserves the latter. He gives two important reasons against the separation of religion and politics. They are:

(i) The separation introduces a dichotomy between the public and private life. For Gandhi, '...political life must be an echo of private life and that there cannot be any divorce between the two' (1986: 375); and

(ii) The separation introduces division, both at the level of thought and reality, and this presents a false picture. Expressing his preference for a holistic world view, he says, '...the word "political" is inclusive. I do not divide different activities—political, social, religious, economical—into watertight compartments. I look upon them all as one indivisible whole each running into the rest and affected by the rest'. (1986: 408)

Religion and Orthodoxy-Tradition

However, Gandhi's positive attitude towards religion does not commit him to carry the burden of the complete religious tradition. In many instances, he clearly unloads this burden. For instance, Gandhi says:

(i) I worship Rama, the perfect being of my conception, not a historical person...[however] the story of a *shudra* having been punished by Ramachandra for daring to learn the Vedas I reject as an interpolation (1950: 10);

(ii) 'The stories told in the Puranas are some of them most dangerous, if we do not know their bearing on the present conditions' (1950: 23);

(iii) ...even if the practice of animal sacrifice be proved to have been a feature of Vedic society, it can form no precedent for a votary of *ahimsa* (1950: 49); and,

(iv) Words have, like man himself, an evolution, and even Vedic texts must be rejected if it is repugnant to reason and contrary to experience. Thus, so far as I understand the *sastras*, I think that there is no authority in them for untouchability as we understand it today. (1950: 286)

Further, he says:

I do not hold that everything ancient is good because it is ancient. I do not advocate surrender of God-given reasoning faculty in the face of ancient tradition. Any tradition, however ancient, if inconsistent with morality is fit to be banished from the land. Untouchability may be considered to be an ancient tradition, the institution of child-widowhood and child-marriage may be considered to be ancient tradition, and even so many an ancient horrible belief and superstitious practice. I would sweep them out of existence if I had the power. (1950: 290)

Thus, in Gandhi, the notion of religion or spiritualism is not static, nor is it mere orthodoxy, it is dynamic. Ashis Nandy rightly characterizes Gandhi as a critical traditionalist (1989). (For more on various interpretations of Gandhi by A.L. Basham, Richard Lennoy, A. K. Saran, Ashis Nandy, Bhikhu Parekh, see my earlier work [1996]).

RELIGION AND STATE-POWER

Gandhi distinguishes politics from state and power. Political power, says Gandhi, is a means for reform, not an end in itself. He says,

If then I want political power, it is for the sake of the reforms for which the Congress stands. Therefore, when the energy to be spent in gaining that power means so much loss of energy required for the reforms, as threatened to be the case if the country is to engage in a duel with the Mussalmans or Sikhs, I would most decidedly advise the country to let the Mussalmans and Sikhs take all the power and I would go on with developing the reforms. (1986: 400)

While admitting that 'there are certain things which cannot be done without political power,' he, however, says that ' but there are numerous other things which do not at all depend upon political power' (1986: 413). He identifies Charkha Sangh, Gramodyog Sangh, Harijan Seva Sangh, Talimi Sangh as inseparable aspects of real politics. He warns that there is a need to 'keep the Sangh untouched by the politics of power and groupism. We have to work in studied silence. That alone would be the beginning of real politics'.[20] (1986: 441)

Thus distinguished both from orthodoxy and state power, Hindu religion to Gandhi stands for a message not of physical might, but a message of love. 'Our religion', says Gandhi, 'is based upon *ahimsa*, which in its active form is nothing but love, love not only to your neighbours, not only to your friends but love even to those who may be your enemies' (1986: 393). Religion, to Gandhi, is not a dogma. It stands for a belief in an ordered moral government of the universe (1986: 391), for truth, non-violence (1986: 373). He pleads for 'introducing charity, seriousness and selflessness in our politics' (1986: 377). Thus Gandhi, in sharp contrast to Savarkar, appeals for spiritualizing politics, as a result making it softer.

Thus defined, it is this notion of religion that Gandhi seeks to use to transform the domain of politics. In this respect Gandhi remains an important critique of modernity and the primacy of the political thesis, which is crucial to modernity. This new definition of politics in important respects is different from Savarkar's ideas. Both Savarkar and Gandhi rejected the separation of religion and politics. However, our reading of Gandhi should not stop at this commonality, as it often does. We must also highlight the fact that Gandhi rejected not only the separation of religion and politics but also Hindutva. Thus, it is not simply appropriate to club Gandhi and Hindutva together.

To conclude, this chapter highlighted the radically different views held by Savarkar and Gandhi on religion and politics as a result of taking opposite directions in overcoming the separation between religion and politics. This places the two in opposite camps. While Savarkar sought to politicize religion, Gandhi pleaded for spiritualizing politics. Recognizing this difference would enormously help in articulating, and understanding the larger tensions engulfing contemporary Indian society and possibly in proposing realistic recommendations to combat communalism through making a case for the Gandhian option, particularly to wean away those who are on the borders of Hindutva.[21,22]

NOTES

1. Anthony Parel in his introduction to *M.K. Gandhi: Hind Swaraj and Other Writings* says:

   It is difficult to estimate the extent of Savarkar's role in the formulation of the philosophy of *Hind Swaraj*. D. Keer, the biographer of both Gandhi and Savarkar, goes so far as to claim that it was written in response to Savarkar. This is clearly an exaggeration, but there is definitely some truth in it. However, that may be, during the later decades the ideological gap between the two only widened. (1997: xxvii)

2. Bilgrami, however, has taken a U-turn in his subsequent interpretation of Gandhi. According to him, a standard and entrenched reading of Gandhi interprets him as maintaining that the search for truth was the goal of life, and since one cannot be sure of having attained the truth, use of violence to enforce one's own view of the truth was sinful. If one goes by this interpretation of Gandhi, one loses sight of the difference between Gandhi's view of non-violence and J.S. Mill's view of liberty. Rejecting this standard interpretation Bilgrami says:

   I have no doubt that Gandhi says things that could lead to such a reading and for years, I assumed that it was, more or less uncontroversially, what he had in mind. After scrutiny of his writings, however, especially his many dispatches to *Young India*, it seems to me now a spectacular misreading. It fails to cohere with his most fundamental thinking. (2002: 82)

3. Enlightenment is an emancipatory project. It, says Kant, 'is man's emergence from his self-incurred immaturity' (1991: 54). Certainties, rationality, individual autonomy, freedom are some of the major aspects constituting Enlightenment. Habermas sees in it a communicative inter-subjective

rationality. Alasdair MacIntyre (1985) equates Enlightenment with fact-value distinction, and Charles Taylor, who says that this distinction is 'the most serious and fundamental claim that arises out of the new conception of modern freedom', endorses this. Further, in another place, Taylor identifies the three malaises of modernity. They are: (i) 'The fear...about what we might call a loss of meaning, the fading of moral horizons...'; (ii) 'the eclipse of ends, in the face of rampant instrumental reason'; and (iii) '...a loss of freedom' (1991: 10). Foucault contests the characterization of modernity 'in terms of consciousness of the discontinuity of time: a break with tradition, a feeling of novelty' (1984: 39). To him, 'Modernity is the attitude that makes it possible to group the "heroic" aspect of the present: modernity is not a phenomenon of sensitivity to the feeling of present: it is the will to "heroize" the present'. (1984: 40)

4. The main thrust of my present work is to focus on the available grounds of difference between contemporary Indian philosophers. By way of clearing the path towards this I have criticized the interpretations of Partha Chatterjee, Sumit Sarkar, Akeel Bilgrami, and others. Similarly I have found some useful ideas and arguments in the writings of Ashis Nandy and T.N. Madan. I have, given the task before me, not been able to engage with their writings in a substantive philosophical debate here. However, I have elsewhere engaged in detailed discussion with Partha Chatterjee in my 'Problematising Nationalism' (1993); with Ashis Nandy in 'Internal Project of Modernity and Post-colonialism' (under communication) and 'West' (2005); and with Javeed Alam in my 'Secularism and Time' (2000). I am presently working on a manuscript which critiques the philosophical foundations, particularly the problem with the tense, inhabited by Indian social scientists which includes the above essays.

5. Hindutva, which is a radically modified version of Hinduism, is installed against the minorities by road rolling the internal differences amongst different communities. While Nandy's critique of Hindutva is sensitive to the transformation processes within the religion, there are others who have not paid attention, which is a serious mistake that has political consequences.

6. Partha Chatterjee, however, contested whether secularism is an adequate and even appropriate ground on which the political challenge of Hindu majoritarianism can be met (1994). I agree with Chatterjee on this. However, my sources and arguments for contesting the same are different.

7. Suresh Sharma's essay entitled, 'Savarkar's Quest for a Modern Hindu Consolidation' (1996) also discussed attempts at articulating the new ideals of Hindu.

8. In his book entitled, *Hindutva: Exploring the Idea of Hindu Nationalism* (2003), Jyotirmaya Sharma traces the lineage of Savarkar to Dayananda Saraswati through Sri Aurobindo and Swami Vivekananda. Political accuracy apart, such an effort displays the tendency to think in terms of historico-causal lines, eclipsing the possibility of jerks of contestation. At political plane, it

facilitates the appropriation of these personalities by the Hindutva ideology, whose opponents consequently feel weakened and even threatened.

This apart, there is a need to think about the theoretical gain that might accrue from such a lineage-oriented approach. One of the central themes of the present work is to draw attention to the intellectual fertility that can be yielded by juxtaposing the thinkers who hold apparently and even deceptively similar views, the case in point for instance being between Swami Vivekananda and Mahatma Gandhi debate in the previous chapter.

Apart from these, Sharma's work, however, throws greater light on the idea of Hindutva.

9. Here it is important to recall that while Partha Chatterjee puts Gandhi in an order where he is preceded by Bankim and succeeded by Nehru, thereby relegating their significant differences to secondary status and highlighting the ascending process of nation-building, Akeel Bilgrami, on the other hand, places Gandhi together with Hindutva thereby flushing out or burying their significant differences between them.

10. Further, the basic prerequisite of democracy is individualism. Democracy with individualism is an effective democracy but is not compatible with pluralism. Democracy with community considerations is a diluted form of democracy but this possibly is compatible with pluralism. In the second form, democracy, though not in principle but as a matter of fact, tends to bolster the possibility of a fixed majority, where community and cultural terms enter into the making of democracy, whereas the democracy that is sustained by individualism, where individuals express their own interest rather than community preferences, facilitates the possibility of a shifting majority. As already pointed out, this form of democracy cannot promote pluralism. The overriding consideration of both reason and individualism, given the inner logic of the Enlightenment, tends more towards homogeneity and is incompatible with pluralism.

11. In contrasting the Enlightenment obsession with unity and its rejection of pluralism in both Western and Indian societies, I am not discounting the oppression and evil in these societies. However, our terms of negotiating the traditional oppression must be different from those of the modern oppression.

I think it was Mahatma Gandhi who negotiated both traditional oppression and modern without clubbing them together. His critique of modernity did not force him to embrace tradition. He accepted the pre-modern societies but sought to bring structural changes in these societies.

12. In contrast, Javeed Alam in his book entitled, *India: Living with Modernity* (1999) makes an interesting move as a response to the postmodern attack, thus saving modernity from direct shocks, and subsequently, formulating a revised and a more acceptable version of modernity. In the process Javeed draws our attention away from the mainstream Enlightenment thinkers such as Descartes and towards less controversial thinkers such as Spinoza.

This attempt at pluralizing modernity can yield interesting and less oppressive options for Indian politics.

13. However, Hindutva can be criticized by demonstrating the desirability of liberal political ideals. In addition, this desirability might justify the homogeneity. However, this has to be stated differently, which has not been done by Sarkar. Of course, this does face the problem of ethical monism. One might, for example, discard all the objectivist schools and make a case for pluralism, away even from relativism. For details on this, see my earlier work (1995a).

14. Many of the statements of Savarkar and Mahatma Gandhi are contextual. While it would have been very useful to work out a methodology to decontextualize these contexts, this will not be undertaken here.

15. Here I am not checking the historical truth of Savarkar's statements. My main concern is to analyse his depiction of the idea of Hindutva.

16. Also, Tejaswini Niranjana, in the context of discussing the emergence of new nationalism in Manirathnam's film *Roja* says: 'That is what I was getting at in asserting that Rishi's [the hero in the film] nationalism is not anti-Western but anti-Muslim. Perhaps I should put it differently: the new nationalism is *pro*-Western and is thus, by definition, anti-Muslim' (1994: 1299). Here it may be noted that the new nationalism (of Hindutva) need not necessarily be anti-Western and in fact, by its historical making is the product of, and therefore resembles Western modernity. Rishi Kumar's computer science background in the film goes very well with Savarkar's fascination for modern science and industry. In a manner of speaking, Rishi Kumar in the film realizes Savarkar's ideals. This is not to underplay the differences between modernity and Hindutva. I am only trying to highlight their oft-forgotten commonality.

Regarding Hindutva being *pro*-Western, but by definition anti-Muslim, given the historical relation between Hindutva and modernity, it is not unnatural that the former is pro-Western. However, one must note here that there are indeed nationalisms within the Swami Vivekananda framework, which are not anti-Western but also not anti-Muslim. In my earlier work (1993) I have retained the tension—governed by proximity and difference—between the ideology of Hindutva and modernity.

17. If Indian liberalism does not share these assumptions of the Enlightenment, then the contents of Indian liberalism need to be elaborated. Further, if one has to make out a case for that form of government that positively protects the rights of the minorities, then those instances have to be elucidated. Partha Chatterjee attempts this in his essay (1994) where he has made out a case for democracy protecting the rights of minorities by evoking the notion of tolerance. This is also the major argument of Rajeev Bhargava in his essay (1994). Alternatively, we may also have to set different terms to negotiate the politics of Hindutva. This may sometimes require going beyond the Enlightenment framework. This sacrifice may be necessary, given the

dangerous politics of Hindutva. We can also look at alternative ways of critiquing Hindutva. One of the important critiques in this direction is suggested by Ashis Nandy (1989). It is in this direction that I too look at the philosophy of Gandhi.

18. Following Said, I treat Gandhi as not an antiseptic thinker, I am only highlighting one and perhaps the dominant aspect in him although it is true that there are many passages in his writings that give rise to radically different kinds of interpretation. For instance, Gyanendra Pandey quotes the following statements of Gandhi to criticize him. Gandhi maintained:

> Nationalism is greater than sectarianism. And in that sense we are Indians first and Hindus, Musslmans, Parsis, Christians after. (26 January, 1922)

And,

> The brave [Ali] Brothers are staunch lovers of their country, but they are Musslmans first and everything else afterwards. It must be so with every religiously-minded man. (24 September 1921)

The non-antiseptic type has its own casualties; these are some such in Gandhi, which have to be owned rather than dismissed. These vulnerabilities too constitute a part of Gandhiana. Having accepted this, what I propose in this chapter is a desirable version which is contemporarily relevant. There may be many other undesirable ones in Gandhi which I surely do not endorse but at the same time they do not allow me to totalize him.

19. Here it is interesting that a contrasting portrayal of the British-modern civilization by Savarkar and Gandhi underlies their rejection. Savarkar attributes to the West/British the use of religion for promoting their political interests. This he endorses with admiration and thus formulates the ideology of Hindutva in proximity to modernity. Gandhi, on the other hand, sees in modernity an absence of religion. He rejects not only the ideology of Hindutva but also the politics of modernity. Here it may not be an exaggeration to say that the root of the basic difference between Savarkar and Gandhi lies in their reading of the modern West. In other words, the local or national differences between Gandhi and Savarkar are enacted against the backdrop of the West.

20. Partha Chatterjee (1986) may be right in arguing that though Gandhi vehemently opposed the idea of civil society—an aspect of modern civilization—he, however, made the emergence of the Indian nation-state possible.

However, the following possibilities available in Gandhi may be taken into consideration before making this conclusive statement:

(i) Gandhi may not have rightly read the designs of the modern civilization, which he was critiquing. Hence, his critique of modernity is not well-informed. (However, I personally believe that Gandhi's critique of modernity is one that cannot be easily co-opted. And an investigation into the validity of Gandhi's critique of modernity, though possible, is outside the scope of this chapter.) This eventually made the programmes of civil society to co-opt Gandhi.

(ii) Having realized the co-option, Gandhi might have subsequently punctuated his notion of politics by clearly distinguishing it from both state and power. This latter phase of Gandhi is equally significant. This phase, however, would remain outside Partha Chatterjee's analysis of Indian nationalism.

21. This option in fact is the dominant view of the civil society in India, particularly in the villages, given the fact that communalism is largely an urban phenomenon, though presently it is also threatening to spread towards the villages, mostly engineered by the Hindu right.

22. Communalism has both regional and global dimensions within it. It evokes local symbols and it is a negative reaction to the universalist project of modernity. Contrary to general belief, communalism does not exist between two communities. From this it does not follow that there is always communal harmony amongst communities. The community conflicts must be distinguished from communal conflicts. One of the distinguishing factors is that in a conflict between two communities, there is at least an initial clarity partly facilitated by the layered distance amongst communities. While there are many overlappings amongst communities, there is nevertheless clarity about the differences regarding their community identities. In contrast, most of the communal conflicts, at least in the beginning, are governed by confusion and chaos. Further, this is largely an urban phenomenon. Raw material for communalism comes from those who have left their communities, immigrated to the urban centres, incorporated features of individualism, and along the way had doubts about these developments. I think it is this uncertain psychological state coupled with the inevitability of the present, which they are not ready to leave, that makes them nostalgic about their community's past. It is this situation of a psychological trap, which in a selective manner makes him or her create second-order community identities, which are largely imaginary, and are quite different from their earlier communities. This uncertainty is at the root of the confusion and chaos that one sees in communal conflicts. These second-order communities do not fully and completely tally with the first-order communities. It may be true that subsequently, due to the former's visibility and articulation, they do make inroads into the first-order communities. However, it is necessary to maintain this distinction. Therefore, this phenomenon is a mixture of both individualism and communities. With this background in mind, let us look into discussions on communalism in India.

■

CHAPTER FOUR

Sri Aurobindo and Krishnachandra Bhattacharyya

Relation between Science and Spiritualism

S ubsequent to the discussion on the relation between religion and politics, this chapter discusses yet another important theme. This too is a relation that concerns contemporary Indian thought, namely, the relation between science (matter) and metaphysics or philosophy (spirit), particularly modern science and the metaphysical aspect of philosophy. As a prelude to the discussion, let me recall some standard accounts of this relation in the West. In the classical period, science was construed as a part of metaphysics and in Aristotle, science was based on philosophy. Aristotle placed science in the area of theoretical sciences and tried to explain it on the basis of philosophical speculation. Thus, in the classical period, science was either founded on metaphysics or at least was a part of it.

However, this relation is inverted in the modern period where philosophy (non-metaphysical) comes to be founded on science. Modern science has shed its dependency on philosophy and has become autonomous. Moreover, this has had a tremendous impact on modern philosophical thinking.[1] Many modern philosophers from Descartes, Hobbes to Logical positivists contributed to this inversion. This dependency of philosophy on science for method has been one of the major themes in the philosophy of science. Popper goes to the extent of claiming that the lack of methodology in philosophy, like in science, is responsible for the lack of progress in philosophy. It is another matter that this dependency of philosophy on science has created its own specific problems.[2] This dependency is also the process through which philosophy became more like science and in the process excluded many areas such as metaphysics and moral philosophy. Thus, the excluded domains of philosophy and the scientific realm have fallen apart from each other. Each was criticized by the other subsequently, and there have been attempts by some to synthesize the two domains, who have argued that both matter and spirit are important, and not in a hierarchy, at least in their own domain. Neither can dispense with the other. This pure theoretical distinction within the West has acquired a geographical or cultural dimension, namely, science or materialism is identified with the West and spiritualism with the East or India. Further, a political bargain was also inserted into this. That is, while the West is perceived as being strong in material progress, India is seen as strong in spiritualism. (The relation as pointed out by Edward Said, is instituted by the British to legitimize the colonial project. If the East is other-worldly, then we will take care of their this world, hence the justification for colonialism on moral and philosophical grounds.) However, the West is not complete without spiritualism and neither is India without materialism, so the West can provide materialism to India and in turn India can give the West its spiritualism. Contemporary Indian philosophers offered this political 'barter' while justifying the claim for granting independence to India. The pioneers in this effort were Bankimchandra Chattopadhyaya, Swami Vivekananda, Sri Aurobindo, and S. Radhakrishnan among others.[3] These thinkers envisaged the desirability of continuity between matter and spirit, and as a corollary, science and metaphysics. While conceding the significance of Western thought, they sought to incorporate it within Indian thought. As part of this, they posited continuity from matter to spirit with some significant modifications, while restoring a higher status to Indian spiritualism. Though there are many thinkers who subscribed to this view, here I shall confine only to Sri Aurobindo who argued for the synthesis between matter and spirit or science and spiritualism.[4] In discussing Sri Aurobindo to represent this position I do not treat him as its author, but a compiler, an icon around whom this point of view is formulated. However, this attempt at synthesizing matter and spirit or science and metaphysics has been completely rejected by Krishnachandra Bhattacharyya. In contrast to the synthesizing attempt, Krishnachandra Bhattacharyya institutes a one-way denial namely, denying metaphysics or philosophy. This contrasting position provides a foundation for another important debate on an important theme within the contemporary Indian philosophy.

SRI AUROBINDO

Before I embark on elucidating Sri Aurobindo's views on the relation between science and spiritualism or matter and spirit, let me clarify that in the way that I have focused on Swami Vivekananda instead of Bankim in an earlier chapter, in this chapter the focus is on Sri Aurobindo instead of Swami Vivekananda though the latter had trodden this path earlier. The reasons are twofold. There is an underlying continuity between Swami Vivekananda and Sri Aurobindo. Acknowledging the impact of Swami Vivekananda on him, Sri Aurobindo says,

I was hearing constantly the voice of Vivekananda speaking to me for a fortnight in the jail in my solitary meditation and felt his presence... The voice spoke only on a special and limited but very important field of spiritual experience and it ceased as soon as it had finished saying all it had to say on that subject. (Mehta 1990: 134)

J.L. Mehta also alludes to the underlying commonality between Swami Vivekananda and Sri Aurobindo when he says that the latter was carrying more effectively to the Western world 'the spiritual message of India...' (Mehta 1990: 153)

The second reason for the choice of Sri Aurobindo is, though Swami Vivekananda has a wide range and a national and international reach, which dictated my choice in the earlier chapters, a theme such as the relation between science and spiritualism, however, needs philosophical sophistication which is more available in Sri Aurobindo than in Swami Vivekananda. Killingley also underlines this point while discussing Vivekananda's attempt at highlighting the differences between the Indian theory of evolution and the Darwinian theory of evolution. He says Aurobindo uses more 'systematically than Vivekananda', the word 'involution' to indicate the process whereby the Divine becomes the manifest world, reserving 'evolution' for the reverse process whereby the world, led by pioneering individuals, is brought back to the Divine. (Killingley 1995: 195)

Now let me turn to Sri Aurobindo who is acquainted with the evolutionist philosophy of the West which to him 'has been the keynote of the thought of the nineteenth century' affecting all its 'sciences', 'thinking', 'moral temperament', 'politics and society'. He attributes to it the victory of the materialistic notion of life and the universe which led to the substitution of the moral idea by the evolutionary world view, the idealist by the economic man. ('Evolution,' Vol. 16, 1972: 225)

Distinguishing biology, which he prefers, from physics, he says that in the former there is from the beginning a stirring of consciousness which progresses and organizes itself more and more for self-expression, whereas physics deals with mechanical laws ('Reason, Science and Yoga', Vol. 22, 1972: 201). He identifies the strength of European thought as lying in 'details' ('The Asian Role,' Vol. 1. 1972: 843); in 'ascertained and tangible scientific truth', ('Is India Civilised?—2', Vol. 14, 1972: 15); in 'its laboriously increased riches of sure and firmly tested scientific organization', in laying an 'enormous stress upon force of personality, upon the individual will, upon the apparent man and the desire and demands of his nature' ('A Rationalistic Critique on Indian Culture 4', Vol. 14. 1972: 87). Lauding the contribution of materialistic sciences he says:

Materialistic science had the courage to look at this universal truth with level eyes, to accept it calmly as a starting-point and to inquire whether it was not after all the whole formula of universal being. Physical science must necessarily to its own first view be materialistic, because so long as it deals with the physical, it has for its own truth's sake to be physical both in its standpoint and method... ('Materialism', Vol. 16, 1972: 252)

This European world view also had its impact on India. Alluding to this outside influence Sri Aurobindo says:

It [European influence] has compelled the [Indian] national mind to view everything from a new, searching and critical standpoint, and even those who seek to preserve the present or restore the past are obliged unconsciously or half-consciously to justify their endeavour from the novel point of view and by its appropriate standards of reasoning. ('The Coming of the Subjective Age,' Vol. 15, 1972: 22)

The neglect of matter and this worldly concern are what it did not do from within and the danger from without lies in reducing everything to this physical world. So the European materialistic world view embodied in the evolutionary theory has been of great influence on both Europe and India. Though very remarkable in its achievements and influences both within and outside Europe, Sri Aurobindo however, points out some serious limitations that surround it. They are:

(i) It is only preoccupied with science. He says:

Science has missed something essential; it has seen and scrutinised what has happened and in a way how it has happened, but it has shut its eyes to something that made this impossible possible, something it is there to express. ('Reason, Science and Yoga', Vol. 22, 1972: 197)

(ii) It further tried to reduce everything to the physical universe. ('Cycle of Society', Vol. 15, 1972: 1)

(iii) It bases its theory on the 'idea of the struggle for life' ('Evolution', Vol. 16, 226–7); vital selfishness of the individual, the instinct and process of self-preservation, self-assertion and aggressive living. ('The Ascent of Life', Vol. 18, 1972:199–200)

(iv) It holds on to the thesis that '...the phenomena of heredity that acquired characteristics are not handed down to the posterity and the theory that it is chiefly predispositions that are inherited....' ('Evolution', Vol. 16, 1972: 226)

(v) The 'idea of a slow and gradual evolution' which 'is being challenged by a new theory of evolution through sudden and rapid outbursts....' ('Evolution', Vol. 16, 1972: 227)

(vi) Its determined thesis of '...rigid chain of material necessity....' ('Evolution', Vol. 16, 1972: 228–9)

(vii) Further, Sri Aurobindo says that the Western idea of evolution is the statement of 'a process of formation, not an explanation of our being. Limited to the physical and biological data of Nature...' ('Involution and Evolution', Vol. 16, 1972: 232) and also for instance,

We speak of the evolution of Life in Matter, the evolution of Mind in Matter; but evolution is a word which merely states the phenomenon without explaining it. For there seems to be no reason why Life should evolve out of material elements or Mind out of living form, unless we accept the Vedantic solution that Life is already involved in Matter and Mind in Life because in essence Matter is a form of veiled Life, Life a form of veiled Consciousness ('The Human Aspiration', Vol. 18, 1972: 3).

To recall, the main limitations of the Western theory of evolution are its preoccupation with the physical world, reductionism, the idea of struggle for existence, its position on heredity, its view that the evolutionary process is a slow and gradual evolutionary process, its deterministic thesis, and the fact that it only presents the formation and does not explain it. In spite of these problems, however, Sri Aurobindo does not reject evolutionary theory, which is true within the materialistic domain. He does not fail to assert, however, that India's strength lies in its 'spiritual or ethical purity of the mind' ('A Rationalistic Critique on Indian Culture 4', Vol. 14, 1972: 91). He says:

In the East, on the contrary, the great revolutions have been spiritual and cultural; the political and social changes, although they have been real and striking, if less profound than in Europe, fall into the shade and are apt to be overlooked...,. ('The Conservative Mind and Eastern Progress', Vol. 16, 1972: 323)

At the same time, he does identify some problems within the traditional Indian world view as well. The spiritual achievement or the occult knowledge was 'confined to a few' and it has not spread to the 'whole mass of humanity'. ('The Supramental Evolution', Vol. 22, 1972: 1) Further, he says:

A few may follow the path of the Yogin and rise above their surroundings, but the mass of men cannot ever take the first step towards spiritual salvation. We do not believe that the path of salvation lies in selfishness. ('Swaraj', Vol. 1, 1972: 700)

Yet another principal reason for the failure of the past attempts in spiritualizing mankind was that the endeavour to 'spiritualize at once the material man by a sort of rapid miracle'. Sri Aurobindo asserts that this can be done, however,

...the miracle is not likely to be of an enduring character if it overleaps the stages of his ascent and leaves the intervening levels untrodden and therefore unmastered. The endeavour may succeed with individuals—Indian thought would stay with those who have made themselves ready in a past existence—but it must fail with the masses. ('Conditions for the Coming of a Spiritual Age', Vol. 15, 1972: 237)

Commenting on the exclusiveness of divine life made available to a few individual seekers and generally keeping away from the life of ordinary men, he says:

A divine life...remains something outside or entirely shut away from the life of ordinary men in the world or unconcerned with the mundane existence; it has to do the work of the Divine in the world and not a work outside or separate from it. ('Perfection of the Body', Vol. 16, 1972: 8)

Another important problem with the traditional Indian view is its neglect or reduction of the physical world. He says that the spiritual life 'sees this world as the kingdom of evil or of ignorance and the eternal and divine either in a far-off heaven or beyond world and life'. ('Three Fold Life,' Vol. 20, 1972: 21) He declares, '...the inward too is not complete if the outward is left out of account' ('Materialism', Vol. 16, 1972: 248). Sri

Aurobindo says, if the old religious cultures were often admirable and 'if they had not been defective, they could neither have been so easily breached, nor would they have been the need of a secularist age to bring out the results the religions had sown' ('Materialism', Vol. 16, 1972: 249). Predictably these defects and shortcomings are absent in the modern thought which 'seeks to prepare a sufficient basis in man's physical being and vital energies and in his material environment for his full mental possibilities' ('Three Steps of Nature', Vol. 20, 1972: 10). So the virtues in the Western thought fill the gaps in the Indian thought and the virtues in the Indian thought fill the gaps in the Western, thus providing a perfect fit for a civilizational amalgamation. In a series of pronouncements he makes a case for the need for such collusion. Elucidating different domains of development he says:

The modern scientist strives to make a complete scheme and institution of the physical method which he has detected in its minute workings, but is blind to the miracle each step involves or content to lose the sense of it in the satisfied observation of a vast ordered phenomenon. ('Involution and Evolution', Vol. 16, 1972: 232–3)

And,

All human energy has physical basis. The mistake made by European materialism is to suppose the basis to be everything and confuse it with the source. The source of life and energy is not material but spiritual, but the basis, the foundation on which the life and energy stand and work, is physical. ('The Brain of India', Vol. 3, 1972: 334.)

Pleading for the fact that the two streams of thought indeed need each other to be complete, he says:

The West has put its faith in its science and machinery and it is being destroyed by its science and crushed under its mechanical burden. It has not understood that a spiritual change is necessary for the accomplishment of its ideals. The East has the secret of that spiritual change, but is has too long turned its eyes away from the earth. The time has now come to heal the division and to unite life and the spirit. ('Ourselves', Vol. 16, 1972: 330)

He says further:

It may well be that both tendencies, the mental and the vital and physical stress of Europe and the spiritual and psychic impulse of India, are needed for the completeness of the human movement. ('Is India Civilised?—2', Vol. 14, 1972: 20)

And, further for him, the evolutionary theories of Europe and India, 'at their best have only been half achievements... Neither Europe nor India nor any race, country or continent of mankind has ever been fully civilized...' ('Is India Civilised?—3', Vol. 14, 1972: 31).[5],[6] Also for him, 'East and West have two ways of looking at the life which are opposite sides of one reality' ('Involution and Evolution', Vol. 16, 1972: 241–2).[7]

The developed opposite sides of East and West, he says, 'will meet from two opposite sides and merge in each other and found in the life of a unified humanity a common world-culture. All previous or existing forms, systems, variations will fuse in this new amalgam and find their fulfilment'. ('Is India Civilised?', Vol. 14, 1972: 18)

In a passage reminiscent of the account of Jarasandha's body, he says:

The two continents are two sides of the integral orb of humanity and until they meet and fuse, each must move to whatever progress or culmination the spirit in humanity seeks, by the law of its being, its own proper Dharma. A one-sided world would have been the poorer for its uniformity and the monotone of a single culture; there is a need of divergent lines of advance until we can raise our heads into that infinity of the spirit in which there is a light broad enough to draw together and reconcile all, highest ways of thinking, feeling and living. That is a truth which the violent Indian assailant of the materialist Europe or the contemporary enemy or cold disparager of Asiatic or Indian culture agrees to ignore.[8] ('A Rationalistic Critique on Indian Culture—4', Vol. 14, 1972: 81)

At another place he says:

In Europe and in India, respectively, the negation of the materialist and the refusal of the ascetic have sought to assert themselves as the sole truth and to dominate the conception of Life. In India if the result has been a great heaping up of the treasures of the Spirit—or of some of them—it has also been a great bankruptcy of Life; in Europe, the fullness of riches and the triumphant mastery of this world's powers and possessions have progressed towards an equal bankruptcy in the things of the Spirit. Nor has the intellect, which sought the solution of all problems in the one term of Matter, found satisfaction in the answer that it has received. ('The Two Negations: The Materialistic Denial', Vol. 18, 1972: 9)

Having justified the need to synthesize or amalgamate the evolutionary theory of Europe, which is materialistic, with the spiritualism of India, Sri Aurobindo elucidates various stages of the synthesized evolutionary process which consists of nine states of descent of the Supreme Spirit into matter. In the reverse direction, it passes through nine stages of ascent.

The stages are: Existence, Consciousness-Force, Bliss, Supermind, Overmind, mind, psyche, life, and matter. (*Life Divine*, Vol. 18, 1972: 264) The stages from mind to matter belong to the empirical world. The stages from Supermind and above are the Supernals and the Divine. The Overmind is the mediator between mind and Supermind which are separated by the veil of maya. The Overmind is something like the witness consciousness (*sâksicaitanya*) of the Vedanta. The first three levels beginning with Existence together constitute the Brahman. Brahman is Being-Consciousness-Bliss (*sat-cit-ânanda*) which splits itself into the three forms. Maya stays between the mind and the Supermind. Maya and the Overmind belong to each other.

As already pointed out, unlike in the evolutionary theory, which fails to explain how life evolves out of matter, Sri Aurobindo assumes that there is spirit or life in the original matter. Moreover, the movement from spirit to matter and vice versa belongs to the very nature of the Absolute; it is maya, which is the power of the Absolute. Both the spirit which is consciousness and maya which is unconscious, are not separate from each other, but belong to each other. The movements of descent and ascent constitute a circular movement of involution and evolution. The aim of man's life is to follow the path of the ascent and rise to the levels of the Supernals one after another. At the higher levels there is no possibility of falsity at all; for there Ignorance and Consciousness are not separated. The Overmind now and then passes on to the mind some great truths which appear like occult truths, inspirations, and intuitions, and cannot be accounted for by the mind. When man rises to the level of the Overmind and becomes one with it, he becomes a Superman. But the Superman of Aurobindo is a yogi, who has surrendered his mind and ego to God with the idea of becoming one with Him. For those who have risen to the higher levels, there is no conflict, no strife. Even if differences are seen there, their unity is also transparent. At the highest level, differences are not seen at all. At that level, the experience is all one, every part of which is completely transparent to every other. Such an experience is integral knowledge to Aurobindo (P.T. Raju, 1985: 545).

Thus synthesized, this attempt is not a routine amalgamation but consists of some serious modifications. For instance, referring to Sri Aurobindo's different use of the word 'evolution', Killingley says that 'it is at odds with earlier uses of the word "evolution"', both in ancient Indian thought and in the Western theory of evolution. He says, for instance,

...ancient Indian thought in English regularly use 'evolution' for the emergence of the world, and of personality, from their original source. Since this source is a unity without parts, while the world contains a multiplicity of phenomena, and personality comprises a number of faculties, this process entails increasing differentiation and complexity, just as does evolution as defined by Spencer. But, in the terminology introduced by Vivekananda and developed by Aurobindo, this is a process of 'involution'. Aurobindo insists that at each stage in evolution, the previous stages are not left behind but taken up. (Killingley, 1995: 195–6)

So there are significant differences in the framework of synthesis undertaken by Sri Aurobindo, thus making more than a mere amalgamation. J.L. Mehta too does not think Sri Aurobindo's attempt to be a mere synthesis but a hermeneutics fusion. Going beyond the idea of mere amalgamation, he maintains:

I wonder if the formula 'science and spirituality' carries us far, for the basic clash here is between two languages, two ways of speaking, that is, thinking, one shaped by three thousand years of Western history and the other bequeathed to us by our own tradition. (Mehta 1990: 148)

Referring to the novel dimensions arising from this activity, he says that the activity of translating from one language to another involves a process where, 'one becomes most keenly and easily aware of the phenomenon of linguistic conflict, and therefore of the spirit and character of each of the two "orders of words", and cultural worlds, that is, of the difference between them'. (Mehta 1990: 156)

And this involves:

The poet brings his native tongue into the charged field of force of another language. He invades and seeks to break open the core of the alien meaning. He annihilates his own ego in an attempt both peremptory and utterly humble, to fuse with another presence. Having done so he cannot return intact to home ground. In each of these hermeneutic motions, the translator performs an action deeply analogous with that of Antigone when he trespasses on the sphere of the gods. (Mehta 1990: 157)

Elucidating this forward march of synthesis or hermeneutic fusion, he says:

As we make the to and fro movement between the parts and the whole, each yields a clearer and more determinate meaning, a meaning moreover, which has nothing to do with the life and mind or times of the author but solely with the matter which finds expression in the text, with an impersonal, intelligible and coherent sense. (Mehta 1990: 166)

Further,

We can now, perhaps only now, after the mediating century or more of an alien decentering agency, take a step back, find the right distance, and begin freely the work of appropriating and coming into true possession of what is our very own, returning home all the wiser for a long voyaging into the alien and the other. No Indian thinker has taken up this double burden on his shoulders with greater determination, and responded to its weight with a matching creative genius than Sri Aurobindo. (Mehta 1990: 164)

Sri Aurobindo's attempt is not mere amalgamation of Western science with Eastern spiritualism but involves serious transformation. To recall, Sri Aurobindo represents a dominant contemporary Indian philosophical attempt which seeks to amalgamate Indian spiritualism with Western materialism. And it is pointed out by Killingley and Mehta that this is not a matter of mere amalgamation.[9],[10]

KRISHNACHANDRA BHATTACHARYYA

Having discussed the synthesizing of materialism and spiritualism against the background of colonialism to which the barter (or double bind of Mehta) was offered, let us now discuss Krishnachandra Bhattacharyya's approach where science 'denies' philosophy. Before that, let me justify my choice of discussing his essay 'The Concept of Philosophy', and not his book *The Subject as Freedom*. For instance, Kalidas Bhattacharyya gives the following reasons to show that Krishnachandra Bhattacharyya's essay represents his mature philosophy for the following reasons. Pointing out the differences between *The Subject as Freedom* and 'The Concept of Philosophy', Kalidas Bhattacharyya says:

These are not difficult theses for those who are acquainted with Bhattacharyya's *The Subject as Freedom*. But there are some additional points—some of which bear even adversely on what he has said in that monograph—which ought to be noted immediately.

First, there is no significant reference, in that monograph, and certainly too no elaboration of it, either to pure self-subsistent object or to pure objective thought or the exact status of metaphysics (and logic) and their relation, on the one hand, to empirical object and empirical thought and, on the other hand, to pure subjectivity and spiritual philosophy.... He has rather shown how directly from science we turn to this latter. Metaphysics, undenied, has not been paid even a fraction of attention he pays to it in his 'The Concept of Philosophy'....

Secondly, what he writes, in this essay, on pure spiritual thinking and its content is not only an improvement, in certain fundamentals, on what he has said on (spiritual) introspection in his *The Subject as Freedom*....

Thirdly, while in *The Subject as Freedom* Bhattacharyya placed the stage 'beyond introspection' under the class *spiritual subjectivity*, here in his 'The Concept of Philosophy', he understands the *absolute* as the content of a grade of thought which is *no longer spiritual*, the reason being that the content here—the absolute—has primarily to be called truth rather than reality and truth is as much qualitatively distinct from reality as reality from self-subsistent object: while reality is all subjective, truth is neither subjective nor objective. (1975: 187–92)

This is the reason for me to discuss his essay apart from the other reason, namely, it clearly articulates the relation between science and philosophy. Krishnachandra Bhattacharyya in this essay distinguishes four grades of thought—empirical, pure objective, spiritual, and transcendental. He classified the empirical thought under science and the other grades of thought under philosophy. Empirical thought is a theoretic consciousness of a content involving reference to an object that is perceived or imagined to be perceived, such reference being part of the meaning of the content. In pure objective thought there are contents that are objective but have no necessary reference to sense-perception. The content of the spiritual thought is no object, nothing that is contemplated in the objective attitude. It is subjective and is appreciated in the subjective or 'enjoying' attitude. Transcendental thought is the consciousness of a content that is neither objective nor subjective. He says that the contents of the four grades of thought may be provisionally called fact, self-subsistence, reality and truth. And science deals with fact and others come under 'philosophy'. Further elucidating their distinguishing character he says that fact is spoken as information and understood without reference to a spoken form. It is what need not be spoken to be believed, as speakability is a contingent character of the content of the empirical thought. Fact is always expressible as a judgment of the form 'A is thus related to B'. However, speakability is the necessary character of the content of pure objective thought. In philosophy, the content that is spoken is not intelligible except as spoken. Speaking is not like information and self-subsistence; reality and truth are not expressed in the form of judgment.

Even when they are expressed in judgment, it is only artificial and symbolic. Philosophy for Krishnachandra Bhattacharyya is self-evident elaboration of the self-evident and is not a body of judgments.

The interesting thing here is that having distinguished these different grades of thought, he goes on to institute a sharper antagonistic relation between science and philosophy, by clearly demarcating the borders between science and philosophy, thus moving from distinction to denial.[11] Here let me reproduce a long quotation. He says:

The philosophy of the object requires to be further distinguished from science. Both deal with the object understood as what is believed to be known in the objective attitude as distinct from the subjective, enjoying or spiritual attitude. The object in science, however, is understood as fact and not as self-subsistent... The self-subsistent is an object that has no necessary reference to the perceivable, is not literally expressible in a judgment and is believed only as it is spoken. (1983: 469)

Thus, having distinguished the two, he moves to the denial posture. He says:

The self-subsistent object is a concept of philosophy, and it is not only not a concept of science but may be even denied by science. Science has no interest to formulate the concept of the self-subsistent object; and it apparently believes that the object *must* be knowable or usable. The self-subsistence of the object implies that the object *may be* in its very nature inaccessible to the mind.

To contemplate the object as what would be if there were no subject to know it is to believe that it may be unknowable, that in any case it is not known as of right. Science would not only take this suggestion to be gratuitous but would positively deny it. The notion that truth freely reveals itself and is in itself a mystery or even that it is its very nature to reveal itself would be scouted by science as obscurantist or anthropomorphic. To science, there is nothing in the object to make it known; it is just what is known and though it may be unknown, there is no question of its being unknowable. (1983: 469–70)

After distinguishing science from metaphysics, Bhattacharyya moves on first to say that the former 'may deny' the latter, then asserts that in some important respects, science 'positively' denies philosophy. This ascending in argumentation clearly established the cleavage between science and metaphysics. Reinforcing the cleavage between science and metaphysics, he says:

The implicit belief of science then is that the object is knowable and usable *as of right*. This belief is at least questioned in philosophy to which it is an expression of solipsistic self-sufficiency on the part of the subject. In normal practical life, nature is not consciously exploited as a tool but is negotiated in the primitive spirit of sociableness. It is the arrogant exploitative attitude of science towards the object that provokes a self-healing reaction of the spirit in the form of philosophy or some cognate discipline. The spiritual demand is that nature should be contemplated and not merely used or manipulated. Science even as theory is evolved in a practical interest. What is more significant is that its very intellectual method is practical, being the use of actual or ideal *contrivances* (1983: 470).

This cleavage between science and metaphysics and the idea of denial of metaphysics by science put forth by Krishnachandra Bhattacharyya is in stark opposition to the synthesizing attempts of Swami Vivekananda, Sri Aurobindo, Sarvepalli Radhakrishnan, and many others who ascribed to the view of an amalgamation of matter and spirit or science and philosophy/metaphysics. Bhattacharyya further explicitly rejects these attempts to bring them together. He says:

The relation between science and the philosophy of the object may be brought out by a reference to certain problems which have been wrongly taken to be philosophical.

More specifically, he says:

[i]There is the problem of piecing together the results of the sciences into a world-view. The synthesis wanted is sometimes imagined to be the generalisation of the primary laws of the sciences into more comprehensive laws...

Further, referring to the evolutionary philosophy which for him is distinct from scientific account of evolution, he says:

Metaphysics may discuss the general concept of evolution which is but the concept of life and its materialistic, spiritualistic or other interpretations. For this, however, it does not require to piece together the results of science, all the data needed— matter, life and mind—being presented in the knowledge of oneself as in the body. The details and specific generalizations of science are utilised in the so-called philosophy of evolution not as evidence but as only illustrative material intended for visualizing the metaphysical theory on the subject. The scientific account of evolution is knowledge or hypothesis, the metaphysic of life in relation to matter and mind is believed, if not known, but the so-called philosophy of evolution, so far as it is different from either, is only an organised presentation of the known or supposed facts of evolution *as though* they constituted the history of a single cosmic life. Cosmic life is not known as a fact, but may still be believed as self-subsisting. The single significant history of this life, however, as rounding off the jagged groupings of fact in science and bridging over the gaps left by it, is only imagined, and is understood to be neither self-evident nor verifiable. The significant story of cosmic evolution then is neither science nor philosophy but only a species of imaginative literature.

In addition to rejecting the synthesizing attempts of the contemporary Indian philosophers, though of course without naming them, he further reinforces this cleavage by rejecting another attempt where science is confused with philosophy. He says:

[ii] There is another problem, viz., the formulation of the postulates or structural concepts of science, which used to be regarded as a philosophical problem. Pure physics, for example, was taken by Kant as a branch of knowable metaphysic established by deduction from the *a priori* principles of synthetic knowledge. There is a similar confusion of thought at the present day in the romantic philosophy that has sprung up round the physico-mathematical theory of relativity, although here the confusion is of science with philosophy and not of philosophy with science as in the other case.

He concludes that:

In both, the impassable gulf between fact and the self-subsistent is ignored. The so-called axioms of science are but postulates, the formulation of which is the work of science itself. The postulates are hypothesis of a kind which are intended not for the anticipation of facts, but for the organization of them into a system. They admit of rival hypothesis and may be rejected though not as contradicted by fact, but only as clumsier and less expeditious to work with than the rival hypothesis. Again, there is no passage from a postulate of science to a concept of the object in itself. (1983: 470–2)

Here it is interesting to note that like in Advaita where Brahman is posited to be the only real and the rest is maya, and the former denies the latter, Krishnachandra Bhattacharyya seems to be using the same strategy though in an inverted form and maintains that science denies the spirit. That is, whereas Sankara rejects matter as maya, Krishnachandra Bhattacharyya ascertains that science (matter) denies philosophy (spirit). Retrospectively speaking, the difference in who denies whom depends upon the dominant position but ultimately the result may be the same when the contexts are neutralized. So there is a comparison and contrast between Krishanachandra Bhattacharyya's idea and Sankara's Advaita. In my assessment while rejecting the attempts of Western philosophers like Kant and Hegel, Bhattacharyya also repudiates the attempts of contemporary Indian philosophers such as Sri Aurobindo. It is this posture that enormously interests me. Krishnachandra Bhattacharyya is forthright in envisaging the opposition and the cleavage between philosophy and science.[12] And this is in direct opposition to the view of Sri Aurobindo. These two important aspects have previously eluded the attention of scholars. For instance, referring to the four grades of thought, Herbert Herring in his 'Krishna Chandra Bhattacharyya's Concept of Philosophy' (1992), says:

Out of these four grades of theoretic consciousness, empirical thought is the realm of the sciences, whereas pure objective, spiritual and transcendental thought are the realms of philosophy. Accordingly we have three branches or disciplines of philosophy, these being in escalating order: philosophy of the object, i.e. metaphysics and logic; philosophy of the subject, i.e. epistemology; and philosophy of truth amounting to transcendental consciousness or consciousness of the transcendent. (1992: 4)

Here it is necessary to note that Herring does not recognize the point that Krishnachandra Bhattacharyya makes regarding the denial of philosophy by science.[13] He merely states that there are four grades of thought and the novel and radical view of Krishnachandra Bhattacharyya with regard to the relation, particularly between philosophy and science, eludes his attention. It must be noted that the active denial of philosophy by science also eludes the attention of Kalidas Bhattacharyya too who only takes cognizance of the difference in this essay showing how 'directly from science we turn' to philosophy. However, Sanat Kumar Sen, another interpreter of Krishnachandra Bhattacharyya, acknowledges this difference between science and philosophy while identifying the difference between the literal and symbolic. He says:

In distinction from literal thought he speaks of these as 'symbolistic thought' and distinguishes the sub-grades of pure objective, subjective and transcendental thought. Embedded in this distinction between literal and symbolistic thinking or in the meanings of 'thinking' and 'speaking' is Bhattacharyya's distinction between science and philosophy, which is not only very original but also highly plausible. Therefore, a critical appreciation of the distinction and relation between thinking and speaking, as conceived by him, is worth undertaking. (Sen 1980: 337)

Later he says:

The distinction between literal or empirical thought and symbolistic thought enables Bhattacharya to demarcate the field of philosophy from that of science or commonsense. (Sen 1980: 338)

Further he says:

Through this *distinction* he has attempted a clear *demarcation* of the field of philosophy from that of science. That this thesis is very original and plausible, and goes a long way in satisfying the much-needed self-identity and self-defence of philosophy may not be disputed. (Sen 1980: 345, emphasis mine)

Here Sen only sees the distinction between science and metaphysics and fails to take cognizance of Bhattacharyya's later idea, that of the denial of metaphysics by science and the cleavage between them. However, S.S. Antarkar goes one step ahead and recognizes the fact that Krishnachandra draws a sharp distinction between philosophy and science. He says:

KCB draws a *sharp distinction* between science and philosophy, though he regards both as forms of theoretic consciousness. (1992: 177, emphasis mine)

Here let me emphasize that Krishnachandra Bhattacharyya not only draws a sharp distinction between science and philosophy but also goes further and declares that the former denies the latter. Here, while agreeing with Sen on the originality of Bhattacharyya, I would like to go beyond the identification of 'difference' (Sen) and 'sharp distinction' (Antarkar) between science and philosophy and lay bare the denial of the latter by the former.

Further, D.P. Chattopadhyaya, while acknowledging the distinction made by Krishnachandra Bhattacharyya, criticizes him in his essay entitled, 'The Concept of Freedom and Krishna Chandra Bhattacharyya'. He says:

This formulation of the different faces of the highest reality does not require KCB to deny the distinction, for example, between objective fact and psychical fact. On the contrary, it is necessary for him in order to relate his own concept of philosophy to the natural sciences and thus to enrich the former and unify the latter. (1992: 19)

Further, Chattopadhyaya suggests that 'KCB's concept of freedom is not inconsistent with science, at least not in principle....' (1992: 39). Here let me only point out that Chattopadhyaya attributes to him the views of Sri Aurobindo, which he vehemently opposes. That is, while Chattopadhyaya, accepting the difference between science and philosophy, advocates the need for the two to 'relate', 'enrich', or 'unify', each other, Krishnachandra Bhattacharyya takes these differences towards denial of metaphysics by science. However, there is a merit in Chattopadhyaya as he does at least implicitly consider Krishnachandra Bhattacharyya's view regarding the antagonism between science and metaphysics. But, in what may be considered as an instance of hermeneutic violence, Chattopadhyaya says that, 'contemporary thinkers like Sri Aurobindo and KCB never fail to take note of what we call the empirical or scientific world (*samsāra*)' (1992: 39).[14, 15] This goes against the very tenor of Krishnachandra Bhattacharyya's work.

Though Chattopadhyaya recognizes Krishnachandra Bhattacharyya's denial posture, he makes a false conflation between him and Sri Aurobindo. Apart from the problems in the nature of his argumentation for my present purpose this exercise of conflation—at times very unconscious in nature and against the contemporary background of colonialism and the efforts of nationalism—this is yet another instance of collapsing significant differences which in turn can provide resources for an active debate. While at one level, this is a necessity as it possibly contributes to the considerations of unity and togetherness, it can also result in a tame and monotonous surrender of fertile difference to unity.

Now let me turn to another neglected aspect of Krishnachandra Bhattacharyya, namely, the difference with the contemporary Indian philosophers like Sri Aurobindo, on which a debate can be formulated. Though these are two diametrically opposite views in understanding the relation between philosophy and science which provide sufficient ground for further philosophizing on this relation, thus highlighting the novel contributions of philosophers like Krishnachandra Bhattacharyya, there are those like S.S. Antarkar who credit Krishnachandra Bhattacharyya rather inaccurately. He says in his 'Krishna Chandra Bhattacharyya's Theory of Value':

Krishna Chandra Bhattacharyya (KCB) is one of the most original twentieth-century Indian philosophers and one of the most insightful constructive interpreters of the classical Indian thought. (1992: 175)

For me the ingenuity of Krishnachandra Bhattacharyya lies more in formulating a counter position to the dominant emerging attempt at positing continuity between matter and spirit. Here it may be noted that Bhattacharyya must be credited not merely for a constructive interpretation of classical Indian thought but also an active repudiation of contemporary thought of other philosophers like Swami Vivekananda and Sri Aurobindo who sought to establish the synthesis of matter and mind, science and spiritualism.

Yet another important interpreter of Krishnachandra Bhattacharyya's philosophy, K. Bagchi, identifies his creativity and says:

Professor Bhattacharyya's task was thus vastly different from, and more complex than, the task of those who, at the turn of the century of British rule in India, contented themselves with just comparing and contrasting Indian and Western philosophical concepts: important as such work undoubtedly was, all that it amounted to was writing *history* of philosophy. The much-needed creative reaction to Western thought was possible on the part of Professor Bhattacharyya because, while he did react with a *traditional* mind (if we may say so), he did not continue *traditionalism*. As a true philosopher who does not ignore his historical milieu but on the contrary makes history *contemporary*, Professor Bhattacharyya exploited the big jolt that Indian mind received through the West by trying to formulate, *initially in Western terms*, the logic of the notions or concepts of Indian thought and *then* bring out the *differentia* of that logic. Only thus is one's mentality restored to oneself, only thus is any *originality* in thought possible. (1981: 19)

Krishnachandra Bhattacharyya's contribution in my view lies not only in providing a strong critique of the West, more specifically of modern Western philosophy, but equally and in my reckoning more than equally, in taking on the contemporary Indian philosophical formulations, particularly those attempts at synthesizing matter and spirit or the West and the East.

To conclude, there are two contrasting perspectives on the relation between matter and mind in contemporary Indian philosophy and this has eluded the attention of the scholars till now, which I attribute to the non-availability of the philosophy of difference in current times. Here let me point out that the difference that I am referring to is not the difference that postmodernists are highlighting.

NOTES

1. Charles Taylor maintains that changes in science need not have total impact on morality. While explicating such assumption in MacIntyre he says:

We might think that there are sufficient grounds to reject Aristotle's teleology once natural science has made the crucial transformation described as 'the mechanization of the world-picture', wrought by Galileo, Descartes and their successors. This seems radically to undercut teleological accounts in general, and in particular in biology. MacIntyre mentions the dependence of Aristotle's ethical views on his 'metaphysical biology'. But this is not so. The notion that human beings have something like a telos *qua* human can be separated from the thesis that everything in nature belongs to some class or other, whose behaviour is explained by some Form or Ideas. Because we no longer explain the movements of stars and stones teleologically does not mean that we cannot explain human in these terms. (1994: 17)

2. Particularly, problems arising when philosophy is founded on science. Philosophical theories are criticized or even outdated but are perhaps not completely rejected. Hobbes is a good example in discussing the relation between philosophy and science. The traditional interpreters of Hobbes maintained that his political philosophy is founded on Galileo's Resolutive-compositive method. Commenting on this Richard Tuck shows that both Richard Peter (Peters' *Hobbes*)' *Hobbes* (1956) and J.W.M. Watkins' *Hobbes's System of Ideas: Essays in the Political Significance of Philosophical Ideas* (1965) have demonstrated the impact of scientific intervention in Hobbes's political philosophy. To quote Tuck:

> First, that Hobbes's political theory was intimately connected with his general scientific philosophy. Second that his scientific method was the same as Galileo's, which was in turn a well established principle of scientific enquiry...namely, the so-called 'resolute-compositive method'. And third, that this was a method of empirical inquiry designed to elicit a moral or political science in the modern sense— something which could be used to explain human social behaviour. Few people [other than those in the second of the post-Kantian tradition] would now disagree with the first of these propositions. (1985: 218)

Tuck in this context is quick to remind us that Leo Strauss differed from Peters and Watkins regarding the impact of science on Hobbes's political philosophy. He says:

> It is true that Strauss, in his early book on Hobbes, devoted some scholarly effort to breaking the link between Hobbes's scientific writings and his political theory.

However, even Strauss, Tuck adds, later recognized the importance of science in Hobbes's political philosophy. Tuck says:

> ...but given the general argument which...[Strauss] put forward later in Natural Right and History, it is not clear that he needed to make this

break. As we have just seen, an interpretation of the rise of modern science is a key feature of that book. (1985: 218–19)

This dependency of philosophy on science has created problems. For instance, when the mechanistic theory of Galileo and Newton was rejected, Hobbes's political philosophy that is based on these theories was hanging in the air. Subsequently there have been attempts to re-found his political philosophy outside science. For instance, Leo Strauss maintains that the basis of Hobbes's political philosophy is 'self-observation,' (1936); A.E. Taylor argues that it is based on 'moral imperative' (1959); J.H. Warrender demonstrates that it is based on 'the theory of moral obligation'; (1957) and for C.B. MacPherson it is based on 'possessive individualism' (1962).

3. Tagore while admitting the limitation of physical nature and maintaining the spiritual realm to overcome this limitation, however, does not commit himself to synthesizing one with the other like Sri Aurobindo. Instead, he sees them as belonging to different realms. He says:

> What is purely physical has its limits like the shell of an egg; the liberation is there in the atmosphere of the infinite, which is indefinable, invisible. Religion can have no meaning in the enclosure of mere physical or material interest; it is in the surplus we carry around our personality— the surplus which is like the atmosphere of the earth, bringing to her a constant circulation of light and life and delightfulness. (2002: 34)

Further, he says:

> Science urges us to occupy by our mind the immensity of the knowable world; our spiritual teacher enjoins us to comprehend by our soul the infinite Spirit which is in the depth of the moving and changing facts of the world. (2002: 131)

And,

> Truth is the infinite pursued by metaphysics; fact is the infinite pursued by science.... (2002: 133)

Though Tagore does not commit, like Sri Aurobindo, to the synthesizing attempt, Killingley wrongly attributes this to him by clubbing them together, when he says:

> The idea was taken up by Aurobindo Ghose, and persists today. Rabindranath Tagore in his lectures on *The Religion of Man*, combined evolutionary and other scientific ideas with the traditional Hindu view of purusa as the starting-point and goal. (1990: 154)

4. Killingley argues, how:

> Hinduism by no means simply incorporated Western evolutionary thought. Indeed, it can be argued that these Hindu thinkers elaborated a framework of interpretation which challenged those notions of

evolution that were usually associated with the writings of Darwin and Spencer. Paradoxically, these thinkers invoked the authority attached to the name of Darwin to [sic] order to achieve this. (1995: 174–5)

5. Keshub Sen holds a similar position. He says:

> But while scientific men stop at the evolution of humanity, we go further and recognize a yet higher stage of development. What is it? Godliness. Out of humanity is evolved divinity, and till that is done our destined evolution is not completed... There are thus four stages through which man has to pass, the inorganic, carnal, human and divine... The highest evolution is regeneration,—the destruction of the lower type of humanity and the evolution of a new species of godly humanity—life divine instead of life human. (in Killingley 1995: 194–5)

6. S. Radhakrishnan says:

> The alleged dialogue between Socrates and the Indian philosopher suggests that for the whole Western tradition man is essentially a rational being, one who can think logically and act in a utilitarian manner. The Western mind lays great stress on science, logic and humanism. Hindu thinkers as a class hold with great conviction that we possess a power more interior than intellect by which we become aware of the real in its intimate individuality, and not merely in its superficial or discernible aspects. (2001: 120)

Later he goes on to fabricate a relation between intellect and intuition. He says:

> The deeper we penetrate, the more unique we become, and the most unique is the most universal.
> Both intellectual and intuitive kinds of knowledge are justified and have their own rights. Each is useful for its own specific purposes. Logical knowledge enables us to know the conditions of the world in which we live and to control them for our ends. We cannot act successfully without knowing properly. But if we want to know things in their uniqueness, in their indefeasible reality, we must transcend discursive thinking. Direct perception or simple and steady looking upon an object is intuition. It is not a mystic process, but the most direct and penetrating examination possible to the human mind. Intuition stands to intellect in somewhat the same relation as intellect stands to sense. Though intuition lies beyond intellect, it is not contrary to it. It is called samyagyñâna, or perfect knowledge. (2001: 140)

7. While there is this adjustment going on between the West and India, there is also a mismatch that has surfaced between Christianity and Darwinism thereby throwing up a domestic problem within the West. Pointing this out, Killingley says:

In this context, 'evolution' held no such terrors for Hindu thinkers as it did for some Christians. Hindus were used to a vast timescale, and to a view of cosmogony as a long process rather than a single creative event; they were used to treating humankind as part of the same continuum of living beings as animals and plants. Indian thinkers such as Bhandarkar and (to a lesser extent) Keshub, who became assimilated into a Western liberal tradition, thereby accepting the notion that the West's destiny was to bring enlightenment to India, contented themselves with pointing to Western ideas as corroborating ancient Indian ones, or as legitimating their own ways of adapting traditional ideas to modern notions of theological truth or of social justice. Others such as Vivekananda and Aurobindo, whose nationalist tendencies involved a rejection of the intellectual hegemony of the West, took evolution out of the hands of the British by identifying with ancient Indian ideas. They claimed further that ancient Indian ideas of evolution were spiritual and therefore superior to those of the West. (Killingley 1995: 196–7)

He adds:

...many Christians in India do not seem to have seen developments in science as inimical to Christianity. They thought of science as a part of European culture from which India would benefit, and as a form of natural revelation which would not conflict with Christianity but would strike a fatal blow at Hinduism. Yet the planned collision between Hinduism and science did not happen. (1995: 178)

8. Bankim Chandra also thought in a similar fashion:

The Guru explains in Dharmatattve.
The day the European industries and sciences are united with Indian *dharma*, man will be god... Soon you will see that with the spread of the doctrine of pure *bhakti*, the Hindus will gain new life and become powerful like the English at the time of Cromwell or the Arabs under Muhammad. (In Partha Chatterjee 1985: 79)

Here it may be pointed out that Sri Aurobindo's attempt is more like a bone-setting by bringing together two different bones, or is it more like a blood transfusion, whether of the same blood group or not, is an open question.

9. Stephen H. Phillips calls Sri Aurobindo a 'mystic empiricist' (1986: 3) and explicates the 'anthro-deanthro' tension in Aurobindo's concept of Brahman. (1986: 150)

10. Peter Heehs, in his essay entitled, 'Shades of Orientalism: Paradoxes and Problems in Indian Historiography' (2003) brings out the stark contrast between nationalist orientalism best exemplified by Sri Aurobindo and the European orientalism both in intent and texture—a contrast that remains unnoticed by Saidianism.

11. Krishnachandra Bhattacharyya's attempt at separating science from philosophy resembles Gandhi's critique of modernity, and modernity's denial of religion. Further, unlike the attempts in the West to relate philosophy and science, the attempts in India by those like Aurobindo and Krishnachandra Bhattacharyya are against the background of colonialism and struggle for independence. Though both are politically sensitive to the contemporary political compulsions, Sri Aurobindo expresses this by establishing continuity between science and spiritualism, whereas Bhattacharyya expresses this by highlighting the denial of spirit by science, thus highlighting the cultural identity as he defends the Advaita position of debunking the empirical reality and installing the reality of Brahman. His stance to demarcate and posit an antagonistic relation between matter and mind is largely Advaitistic.

12. Here it may be appropriate to recall that in one respect J.N. Mohanty does endorse the difference between religion and science when he says:

> ...in my view, religion is not science or super-science. The attempt to justify religion through science is really interpreting science through religion. The danger is on the one hand the pseudo-science (as with American creationism) and on the other, a pseudo-religion. If religion is of any worth, it must be self-sustaining, more fundamentally reality-experiencing than science, but religion of this level will be authentic religiosity and not belief in stories. It must be a way of experiencing the world, oneself, and others.

However, unlike Krishnachandra Bhattacharyya, Mohanty does not see the antagonism of science towards religion. To him,

> Science is neither its [religion's] rival, nor has the power to be an antagonist. The two belong to different levels of discourse. (2002: 49)

However, there is a slight tilt in his position when in his essay, 'Science and Poetry: Apropos a Conversation between Tagore and Einstein', he supports Tagore's stand on objectivity, namely, scientific rationality and logic are human activities. This is in contrast to Einstein who concedes that beauty and religious values are subjective while maintaining that objectivity and scientific truth are independent of the mind. Mohanty says:

> Thus, in my view, science and poetry deliver to us objectivity in different senses, poetry in a stronger sense, science in a weaker sense. (2002: 67)

13. Even Kalidas Bhattacharyya, in his long essay entitled, *Presuppositions of Science and Philosophy*, acknowledges that 'K.C. Bhattacharyya has very thoroughly discussed the notion of subjectivity and its being. Vide *Studies in Philosophy*, 'Subject as Freedom' and 'The Concept of Philosophy', he says that 'In this essay we have touched only the fringes of the problem'. (1974: 44)

14. In a very confusing passage in his essay D.P. Chattopadhyaya says:

   ...the Vedântin and philosophers like KCB show admirable ingenuity and dialectical competence to indicate how the immense resources of human consciousness as available in philosophical concepts and theories may help us to break the barrier between theory and practice, between science and non-science. It is interesting to note, in this connection, that most of the Indian philosophers refuse to accept the dramatized distinction between the above pairs of concepts and their cognates. (1992: 38–9)

15. Mrinal Kanti Bhadra in his essay 'Dissociation, Reduction and Subjectivity', says:

   Perhaps, it is not impossible to discover a phenomenological trend in Krishna Chandra Bhattacharya's...philosophical investigations. (1992: 43)

■

Conclusion

A way from Jarasandha's picture, we have these debates which can
provide illuminating grounds to conduct serious discussions in
contemporary Indian philosophy, thus presenting it not as a subdued or
passive ground completely crushed out by colonialism but having resources
to formulate philosophical activity. The discussions in the previous
chapters show how there are important islands of differences on which
debates, though not like the classical ones, may still be held. All the same,
they reveal some core aspects of the classical while reflecting the changing
contemporary aspects and offer a range of different and contrary
perspectives on these changes. These debates neither adhere to the classical
Indian tradition nor do they tamely traverse the path laid out by Western
philosophy. They fall outside both these realms. These debates also dispel
the apprehension raised at the beginning of the book regarding the
absence of debates and regarding the fact that contemporary philosophical
debates in India are not posited directly. These debates do not use the
West as a relay station, though they are certainly informed by colonial
influence, which they have actively negotiated.

Another important aspect of these debates is their larger philosophical
canvas, which takes into consideration the social-political context. That
is, these debates do not merely confine themselves to the abstract
metaphysical, logic or even epistemological problems that largely
surround classical Indian philosophy. They instead show enormous

sensitivity to the immediate political problems of colonialism, nationalism, problems of modernity and tradition, future of nation-state, etc. Yet another feature is their sensitivity to the existing active non-classical Indian plural social realities, which provide numerous resources for making a philosophy of difference, which is quite different from the postmodern notion of difference. That is, philosophy in India[1] is not unaffected by colonialism as claimed by Sri Aurobindo nor is it dead and mummified as bemoaned by Daya Krishna. Contemporary Indian philosophy stands somewhere between these two extremities, a position which is metaphorically reminiscent of Jarasandha's body. However, it is a pity that scholars have not recognized these important sources for debate.

Here let me make some clarifications regarding the terrain of contemporary Indian philosophy. It is a strange mixture of both contemporary Western philosophy and classical Indian philosophy, and it may be necessary to evaluate this strange combination. We might, for instance, first compare it with contemporary Western philosophy. In comparison it is not as rigorous. For instance, in Swami Vivekananda we come across contradictory and inconsistent views expressed on themes such as the West, science, Advaita, the Indian tradition, Islam, and the priestly class. In Sri Aurobindo, we have a better case, but beyond a point, he too becomes loose. Take, for instance, his attempt at synthesizing materialism and spiritualism, as both spiritualism and materialism are not ignorant of each other, but still reduce or concede only dependent status to what they consider secondary. So their denial of each other is not due to their ignorance but have a philosophical basis. Hence, when these incompatible domains are brought together—here I am not suggesting that they cannot be brought together at all—this has to be rigorously supported by arguments, which in comparison to Western philosophy are found wanting. As already pointed out, this state of affairs of contemporary Indian philosophy is not inherent to classical Indian philosophy, which consists of various *dharsana*s, not necessarily six dharsanas. Also philosophical works during the medieval period displayed textual rigour and clarity of thought. So the lack of rigor in contemporary Indian philosophy is peculiar to it.

However, this state of affairs of contemporary Indian philosophy cannot be taken as a conclusion. It is possible to probe further and find alternative criteria for evaluating the importance of contemporary Indian philosophy. One such alternative is available in A.K. Ramanujan when he identifies Western thought as context-free (ideas of a universal human nature) and Indian culture as context-sensitive. Using this seminal though crude distinction, we can examine and lay bare the context for contemporary Indian philosophy. Here in slight modification to Ramanujan I argue that both classical Western and classical Indian philosophies are context-sensitive. For instance, both Plato and Aristotle, especially in their political works, devote a considerable amount of time and space in their works to analysing their context. It is another matter that they seek to overcome their contexts through transcendence and postulated universals. Thus, it is not correct to say that Western philosophy, as a whole, is context-free. So classical Western, classical Indian, and contemporary Indian philosophies are context-sensitive, whereas contemporary Western philosophy is context-free.

However, it is necessary to distinguish the different natures of these contexts. Both classical Indian and Western philosophies exhibit a mutual interaction between their texts (transcendent) and contexts (immanent). They are preoccupied with their contemporaries and even their distant predecessors. In contrast, those with whom contemporary Indian philosophers were preoccupied were also spatially distanced. Further, these do not share the same language. Contemporary Indian philosophers do not have the immediate or distant other from the same social space with whom they can have philosophical debates. Nevertheless, when they speak, the contents are Indian, mostly Indian spiritualism, but their language and form are Western. That is, they talk to the West about Indian themes. So to revise Ramanujan's classification as follows:

For Ramanujan: Western philosophy = Context-free
                    Indian philosophy = Context-laden

Revised:

Contemporary Western philosophy = Direct + Context-free
Classical Indian philosophy = Direct + Context-laden
Classical Western philosophy = Direct + Context-laden
Contemporary Indian philosophy = Non-direct + Context-laden

This makes the discourse of contemporary Indian philosophy complex. It lacks a direct dialogue (non-direct) but at the same time it is context-laden. The lead players in contemporary Indian philosophy being nationalists, their assertions are directed towards India's independence. They are speakers speaking to their colonial masters. Unlike in other kinds of hierarchies, where the speaker generally is the master and the hearer the subject, the precariousness of this hierarchy is that the speaker is the colonial subject and is speaking to his or her ruler. In this inversion of the colonizer as the putative hearer and the colonised as the speaker, the speaker has to speak in the language of the hearer which happens to be English, and this speaking cannot be mere sermonizing. This package happens to promote Indian spiritualism given in exchange for Western materialism. It is another matter that in this barter, the 'other' is largely absent. Though the 'other' is not listening, the speaker has set a reasonable communication stage for speaking. Further, given the background of colonialism, there is a hierarchy between the speaker and the hearer, speaker speaking from below to the politically higher hearer within the ambience of the freedom struggle.

These contextual confabulations are unprecedented in the history of combative battles. The achievement of contemporary Indian philosophy lies in such aspects. Here let us recall the importance of the hearer to recognize the contributions of contemporary Indian philosophy. Referring to the importance of the hearer in the philosophical discourse in the 'classical *systematic* philosophy in India', Kalidas Bhattacharyya says, 'It is almost always—the only exception being Buddhism—understood from the point of view of the hearer' (1985: 178). Further, referring to an important logical system in India, he says, 'Nyaya is consistent in another procedure too. Language it understands throughout as heard, not as spoken, the speaker being understood as only an erstwhile hearer learning language and its meaning from other speakers and now only using them'. (1985: 183). Hearer-centredness, which is so central to classical Indian philosophy, is resurrected here to account for the ingenuous attempt of the contemporary Indian philosophers.[2]

Yet another peculiar feature of classical Indian philosophy is that, driven by the new circumstances of colonialism, it had to freeze diverse classical philosophical schools and form a monolith, which though consisting of various schools, only projects one of its parts, Advaita, as its representative. Advaita is chosen partly because it fulfils the requirements of identity and difference, to make a case for India's independence. However, in this process, even Advaita is modified and then presented. It has to be translated as monism since the West is familiar with the monism of Spinoza and others, and has no concept of Advaita, which literally means non-dualism.

There are certain serious logical differences between monism and non-dualism. Monism is not non-dualism. Monism is one among others like non-dualism, which falls outside dualism. So the positive association between non-dualism and monism is only the result of negative relation, that is, both non-dualism and monism fall outside dualism. Apart from such an association, there does not seem to be any significant resemblance or commonality between monism and non-dualism. The radical difference underlying monism and non-dualism becomes evident when we explicate their subscription and non-subscription to the numerical order. Monism participates in the numerical order: whereas non-dualism refuses to participate in any numerical order including zero in the form of *sunyavada* of Buddhism.

To return to the main argument, Advaita is translated as monism.[3] Herein lays the ingenuity of contemporary Indian philosophy in operating with these larger political requirements of nationalism, and to make contact with an alien hearer.

Along with re-looking both with analytical rigour and comparative spirit at these small but significant issues and problems, it is necessary to restate in a substantial way the entire purview of the contemporary Indian philosophy. This should include bringing into focus a critical understanding of the classical Indian philosophy and Western philosophies and non-partisan critique of colonial context. One way of restating is not to absolve the available intellectual differences amongst contemporary Indian philosophers but nurture them; instead of negotiating the classical Indian philosophy with modern Western philosophy, thus committing to a temporary inequality, it is perhaps advisable to import the relevant themes both from the classical India and contemporary West and process them within the thematic of the contemporary Indian philosophy. All these might help in undoing what Bhima had done to Jarasandha's body, thus restoring natural shape. A rejuvenated contemporary Indian philosophy may reveal not only the complexities of present India but also facilitate a better understanding of the classical Indian philosophy and Western philosophy. This can take us one step further to the achievements effected by earlier contemporary Indian thinkers.

In undertaking this task, this volume is guided by the fact that the task of philosophy is not only to work with ready-made problems as available in philosophical systems—a feature that seems to have guided those who have been preoccupied by already available classical Indian philosophy and modern Western philosophy, more specifically Panini and Chomsky or Nyaya and Russell. Equally important task of philosophy is to formulate new discourses, systematize loose arguments, and explicate in logical terms the scattered insights. We do find in history many such instances where philosophy has embarked on this task. Further, making a similar attempt to formulate an active contemporary Indian philosophy might also make philosophical activity in India today sensitive to the contemporary processes, and assign to it new notions of both autonomy and responsibility, though not necessarily social responsibility.

NOTES

1. Regarding Indian philosophy, Matilal says:

   I have found the expression 'Indian philosophy' puzzling more often than not. For one who has spent most of the life writing books and papers and editing journals on Indian philosophy, this is an odd admission. But one brief look at the titles of the papers presented on the subject, will vindicate the fact that the expression 'Indian philosophy' is utterly ambiguous and genuine doubt is entertained by many as to its exact significance. (2002: 351)

2. However, one of the major preoccupations of postcolonial studies is only within the speaking subject and they do not recognize the importance of the hearer in the discourse. They are preoccupied with, 'how the third-world subject is represented within Western discourse'. (Spivak 1988: 271)

   These studies piloted by Edward Said laid bare the politics and unearthed the modes and motivation surrounding the Occident's representation of the Orient. This, namely, 'representation of other cultures,' 'who writes, or studies the Orient' (1986: 212) continues to preoccupy Said. Merely adding some more to the list he says:

   In these methodological and moral reconsiderations of Orientalism I shall quite consciously be alluding to similar issues raised by the experiences of feminism or women's studies, black or ethnic studies, socialist and anti-imperialist studies, all of which take for their point of departure the right of formerly un- or misrepresented human groups to speak for and represent themselves in domains defined, politically and intellectually, as normally excluding them, usurping their signifying and representing functions, over-riding their historical reality. In short, Orientalism reconsidered in this wider and libertarian optic entails nothing less than the creation of new objects for a new kind of knowledge. (1986: 212)

   Referring to Said's book *Orientalism,* Gayatri Spivak says: 'The study of colonial discourse, directly released by work such as Said's, has, however, blossomed into a garden where the marginal can speak and be spoken, even spoken for. It is an important part of the discipline now' (1993: 56). This also constitutes Gayatri Spivak's criticism of J.S. Mill, Jean Paul Sartre, Julia Kristeva, etc. (1999). The problem surrounding representation also becomes the main focus of attention in her earlier famous essay, 'Can a

Subaltern Speak?' (1988), which Leela Gandhi (1999) has adequately paraphrased. I quote Gandhi:

> Spivak's famous interrogation of the risks and rewards which haunt any academic pursuit of subalternity drew attention to the complicated relationship between the knowing investigator and the (un)knowing subject of subaltern histories. For how, as she queried, 'can we touch the consciousness of the people, even as we investigate their politics? With what voice-consciousness can the subaltern speak?'.... Through these questions Spivak places us squarely within the familiar and troublesome field of 'representation' and 'representability'. How can the historian/investigator avoid the inevitable risk of presenting herself as an authoritative representative of subaltern consciousness? Should the intellectual 'abstain from representation?'...which intellectual is equipped to represent which subaltern class? Is there an 'unrepresentable subaltern class that can know and speak itself?'.... And finally, who— if any—are the 'true' or 'representative' subaltern of history, especially within the frame of reference provided by the imperialist project? (1999: 2)

Following Said, in Spivak and others, representation has become a rallying theme for discussion. Thus postcolonialism succeeded in explicating the politics of representation, exposed that the Orient is a construction, and made a case for self-representation where the 'marginal can speak and be spoken for' (Spivak 1993: 56). In shifting the ground from the Occident as the representing subject to self-representation or from the 'knowing investigator' to the '(un)known subject of subaltern histories', the very status of the postcolonial thinkers came for a closer scrutiny: Where do they belong, whether they belong to this or that side of the pendulum, indeed what is their location?

Though in most of the cases the dimension of the hearer has not been taken into account, we do find some suggestions indicating the hearer dimension in Aijaz Ahmad when he says: 'The issue of assembling and professionalizing a new area of literature, namely, "Third World literature", has arisen primarily in the metropolitan university, in England and North America for the most part...' (1992: 43). And these for him are to be seen as responding to quite specific kinds of pressure by appropriating particular kinds of texts, and by devising a new set of categories within the larger conceptual category of literature as such.

The question of the reader is raised marginally by Matilal when he writes in the preface to his book, *The Navya-Nyaya Doctrine of Negation: The Semantics and Ontology of Negative Statements in Navya-Nyaya Philosophy*:

> From time to time...writing this book I have stopped to ask myself for whom I was writing. Much as I have pondered the question, I have not yet arrived at a satisfactory answer. (1968, p. ix)

Apart from these isolated instances, which are brief and indirect, where the importance of the hearer is raised, the preoccupation within postcolonialism is largely with the domain of self-representation.

3. Regarding problems in translating Advaita as monism, Gayatri Spivak says:

> Whatever the philosophers say, I think it is important that mono—as well as poly—would be mistranslations of *advaita* or *dvaita* that would take away the agility of the popular ethical mindset that makes nothing of this undecidability. Mono is 'un-two-ed', a strange way of saying One! Omni-(science or potence) does not fit into this too well. And the 'two-ed', without a precise authority of a One to stand guard over it, can stand in for an indefinite swarm. Translation of *advaita* and *dvaita* into monism (non-dualism) and dualism has a lot to answer for. (1993: 173–4)

Bibliography

Ahmad, Aijaz. 1992. *In Theory: Classes, Nations, Literature*, Oxford: Oxford University Press.

Alam, Javeed. 1998. 'Indispensability of Secularism', *Social Scientist*, Vol. 26, Nos. 7–8, July–August, pp. 3–20.

_____.1999. *India: Living with Modernity*, New Delhi: Oxford University Press.

Anschutz, R.P. 1963. *The Philosophy of J.S. Mill*, Oxford: Clarendon Press.

Antarkar, S.S. 1992. 'Krishna Chandra Bhattacharyya's Theory of Value', *Journal of Indian Council of Philosophical Research*, Vol. X, No. 1, special issues on The Philosophy of K.C. Bhattacharyya, pp. 175–91.

Aurobindo, Sri. 1972. *Bande Mataram: Early Political Writings 1*, Vol. 1, Pondicherry: Sri Aurobindo Birth Centenary Library.

_____. *The Harmony of Virtue: Early Cultural Writings*, Vol. 3, Pondicherry: Sri Aurobindo Birth Centenary Library.

_____. *Foundations of Indian Culture and the Renaissance in India*, Vol. 14, Pondicherry: Sri Aurobindo Birth Centenary Library.

_____. *The Social and Political Thought*, Vol. 15, Pondicherry: Sri Aurobindo Birth Centenary Library.

_____. *Supramental Manifestation and Other Writings*, Vol. 16, Pondicherry: Sri Aurobindo Birth Centenary Library.

_____. *The Life Divine*, Vol. 18, Pondicherry: Sri Aurobindo Birth Centenary Library.

_____. *The Synthesis of Yoga: Parts One and Two*, Vol. 20, Pondicherry: Sri Aurobindo Birth Centenary Library.

Aurobindo, Sri. *Letters on Yoga: Parts One and Two*, Vol. 22, Pondicherry: Sri Aurobindo Birth Centenary Library.

Bagchi, K. 1981. 'Towards a Metaphysic of Self: Perspectives on Professor Krishnachandra Bhattacharyya's Unpublished Essay on "Mind and Matter"', *Journal of Indian Philosophy*, No. 9, pp. 19–37.

Banga, M.S. 2001. 'Interview', in *India Today*, 19 November.

Berlin, Isaiah and Bernard Williams. 1994. 'Pluralism and Liberalism: A Reply', *Political Studies*, XLI, pp. 306–9.

Bhadra, Mrinal Kanti. 1992. 'Dissociation, Reduction and Subjectivity', *Journal of Indian Council of Philosophical Research*, Vol. X, No. 1, Special issues on The Philosophy of K.C. Bhattacharyya, pp. 43–57.

Bhargava, Rajeev. 1994. 'Giving Secularism Its Due', *The Economic and Political Weekly*, 9 July, pp. 1784–809.

Bhattacharyya, Kalidas. 1974. *Presuppositions of Science and Philosophy & Other Essays*, Visva-Bharati: Centre of Advanced Study in Philosophy.

———. 1975. *The Fundamentals of K.C. Bhattacharyya's Philosophy*, Calcutta: Saraswat Library.

———. 1982. 'Traditional Indian Philosophy as Modern Indian Thinkers View it', in *Indian Philosophy: Past and Future*, Pappu, Rama Rao, S.S and R. Puligandla, eds Delhi: Motilal Banarsidass, pp. 171–224.

———. 1985. 'Some Problems Concerning Meaning', in *Analytical Philosophy in Comparative Perspective*, eds B.K. Matilal and J.L. Shaw, Dordrecht, Holland: D. Reidel Publishing Company, pp. 173–86.

Bhattacharyya, Krishnachandra. 1983. 'The Concept of Philosophy', *Studies in Philosophy*, Vols I and II, ed. Gopinath Bhattacharyya, Delhi: Motilal Banarsidass, pp. 457–79.

Bilgrami, Akeel. 1994. 'Two Concepts of Secularism: Reason, Modernity and Archimedean Ideal', *The Economic and Political Weekly*, 9 July, pp. 1749–61.

———. 2002. 'Gandhi's Integrity: The Philosophy behind the Politics', *Postcolonial Studies*, Vol. 5, No. 1, pp. 79–93.

Bordo, Susan. 1987. *The Flight to Objectivity: Essays on Cartesianism and Culture*, Albany: State University of New York Press.

Brantlinger, Patrick. 1996. 'A Postindustrial Prelude to Postcolonialism: John Ruskin, William Morris, and Gandhism', *Critical Inquiry*, 22, Spring, pp. 466–85.

Browning, Robert. W. 1992. 'Reason and Intuition in Radhakrishnan's Philosophy', in *The Philosophy of Sarvepalli Radhakrishnan*, ed. Paul Arthur Schilpp, Delhi: Motilal Banarsidass, pp. 173–277.

Chatterjee, Partha. 1985. 'The Fruits of Macaulay's Poison Tree', in *The Truth*

Unites: Essays in Tribute to Sameer Sen, ed. Ashok Mitra, Calcutta: Subarnarekha, pp. 70–89.

Chatterjee, Partha, 1986. *Nationalist Thought and the Colonial World: A Derivative Discourse?*, Delhi: Oxford University Press.

———.1994. 'Secularism and Toleration', *The Economic and Political Weekly*, 9 July, pp. 1769–77.

Chattopadhyaya, D.P. 1992. 'The Concept of Freedom and Krishna Chandra Bhattacharyya', *Journal of Indian Council of Philosophical Research*, Vol. X, No. 1, special issues on The Philosophy of K.C. Bhattacharyya, pp. 13–42.

Crowder, George. 1994. 'Pluralism and Liberalism', *Political Studies*, XLII, pp. 293–305.

Dasgupta, S.N. 1982. 'Dogmas of Indian Philosophy', in *Philosophical Essays*, Delhi: Motilal Banarsidass, pp. 208–33.

Descartes, R. 1985. Discourse on Method', in *The Philosophical Writings of Descartes*, Vol. I, trans. John Cottingham, Robert Stoothoff and Dugald Murdoch, Cambridge: Cambridge University Press, pp. 111–51.

Dummett, Michael. 1966. 'Matilal's Mission: A Memorial Address', *Studies in Humanities and Social Sciences*, Vol. III, No. 2, pp. 13–17.

Ebenstein, William. 1972. *Great Political Thinkers*, Calcutta: Oxford and IBM.

Eco, Umberto. 1987 *Travels in Hyperreality*, London: Picador.

Fanon, F. 1977. *The Wretched of the Earth*, Harmondsworth: Penguin Books.

Foucault, Michel. 1984. 'What is Enlightenment?', in *The Foucault Reader*, ed. Paul Rabinow, New York: Pantheon Books, pp. 32–50.

———.1984. 'What is an Author', in *The Foucault Reader*, ed. Paul Rabinow, New York: Pantheon Books, pp. 341–53.

———. 1988. *Technologies of Self: A Seminar with Michel Foucault*, eds Luther H. Martin et al., Amherst: The University of Massachusetts Press.

Gandhi, Leela. 1999. *Postcolonial Theory: A Critical Introduction*, New Delhi: Oxford University Press.

Gandhi, M.K. 1950. *Hindu Dharma*, ed. Bharatan Kumarappa, Ahmedabad: Navajivan Publishing House.

———.1968. *The Selected Works of Mahatma Gandhi: The Voice of Truth*, Vol. 6, ed. Sriman Narayana, Ahmedabad: Navajivan Publishing House.

———. 1976. *Autobiography*, Ahmedabad: Navajivan Publishing House.

———. 1986. *The Moral and Political Writings of Mahatma Gandhi: Civilization, Politics and Religion*, Vol. I., ed. Raghavan Iyer, Oxford: Clarendon Press.

———. 1989. *Hind Swaraj or Indian Home Rule*, Ahmedabad: Navajivan Publishing House.

Gellner, Ernest. 1983. *Nations and Nationalism*, Oxford: Basil Blackwell.

Giddens, Anthony. 1982. *Profiles and Critiques in Social Theory*, London: Macmillan.

Heehs, Peter. 2003. 'Shades of Orientalism: Paradoxes and Problems in Indian Historiography', *History and Theory: Studies in the Philosophy of History*, Vol. 42, No. 2, pp. 169–95.

Herring. Herbert. 1992. 'Krishna Chandra Bhattacharyya's Concept of Philosophy', *Journal of Indian Council of Philosophical Research*, Vol. X, No. 1, special issues on The Philosophy of K.C. Bhattacharyya, pp. 1–12.

Hiriyanna. 1967. *Outlines of Indian Philosophy*, London: George Allen & Unwin, Ltd.

Kakar, Sudhir. 1996. *The Indian Psyche*, New Delhi: Oxford University Press.

Kant, Immanuel. 1991. 'An Answer to the Question: "What is Enlightenment?" in *Kant: Political Writings*, trans. N.B. Nisbet, ed. by Hans Reiss. Cambridge: Cambridge University Press, pp. 54–60.

Keer, Dhananjaya. 1966. *Veer Savarkar*, Bombay: Popular Prakashan.

Kelkar, Ravindra and R.K. Prabhu, eds 1961. *Truth Called Them Differently: Tagore–Gandhi Controversy*, Ahmedabad: Navajivan Publishing House.

Kendal, Willmoore. 1941. 'John Locke and the Doctrine of Majority-Rule', published under *Illinois Studies in the Social Sciences*, 26.(2), pp. 1–139.

Killingley, Dermot. 1990. 'Yoga-Sutra IV, 2–3 and Vivekananda's Interpretation of Evolution', *Journal of Indian Philosophy*, No. 18, pp. 151–79.

―――. 1995. 'Hinduism, Darwinism and Evolution in Late-Nineteenth-Century India', in *Charles Darwin's The Origin of Species: New Interdisciplinary Essays*, eds Amigoni, David and Jeff Wallace, Manchester: Manchester University Press, pp. 174–202.

―――. 1999. 'Vivekananda's Western Message from the East', in *Swami Vivekananda and the Modernisation of Hinduism*, ed. William Radice, New Delhi: Oxford University Press, pp. 138–57.

Krishna, Daya. 1987. (ed.) *India's Intellectual Traditions: Attempts at Conceptual Reconstruction*, New Delhi: Indian Council of Philosophical Research.

―――. 1996. *Indian Philosophy: A Counter Perspective*, New Delhi: Oxford University Press.

Krishna, Daya and A.M. Ghose. 1978. *Contemporary Philosophical Problems: Some Classical Indian Perspectives*, Poona: Indian Philosophical Quarterly Publications.

Krishna, Daya, M.P. Rege, et al. 1991. *Samvâd: A Dialogue between Two Philosophical Traditions*, New Delhi: Indian Council of Philosophical Research.

Kuhn, Thomas. 1959. *The Copernican Revolution*, New York: The Random House.

Larson, G.J and Eliot Deutsche. (eds) 1989. *Interpreting Across Boundaries: New Essays in Comparative Philosophy*, Delhi: Motilal Banarsidass Publishers Pvt. Ltd.

MacIntyre, A.C. 1969. 'Hume on "Is" and "Ought", in *The Is-Ought Question*, ed. W. D. Hudson, London: Macmillan, pp. 35–50.

MacIntyre, Alasdair. 1985. *After Virtue*. London: Duckworth.

MacIver, R.M. 1970. *On Community, Society and Power*, Chicago: University of Chicago Press.

MacPherson, C.B. 1962. *The Political Theory of Possessive Individualism*, Oxford: Clarendon Press.

Madan, T.N. 1999. 'Secularism in Its Place', in *Religion in India*, ed. T.N. Madan, New Delhi: Oxford University Press, pp. 394–409.

Matilal, B.K. 1968. *The Navya-Nyaya Doctrine of Negation: The Semantics and Ontology of Negative Statements in Navya-Nyaya Philosophy*, Cambridge: Harvard University Press.

———. 1986. 'The Logical Illumination of Indian Mysticism', under the series *Oxford University Papers on India*, Vol. I, Part I, eds N.J. Allen, R.F. Gombrish, et. al., New Delhi: Oxford University Press.

———. 1999. *The Character of Logic in India*, eds Jonardon Ganeri and Heeraman Tiwari, New Delhi: Oxford University Press.

———. 2001. *The Word and the World: India's Contribution to the Study of Language*, New Delhi: Oxford University Press.

———. 2002. *The Collected Essays of Bimal Krishna Matilal: Mind, Language and World*, Vol. I, ed. Jonardan Ganeri, New Delhi: Oxford University Press.

———. 2002a. *The Collected Essays of Bimal Krishna Matilal: Ethics and Epics*, Vol. II, ed. Jonardan Ganeri, New Delhi: Oxford University Press.

Mehta, J.L. 1990. *Philosophy and Religion: Essays in Interpretation*, New Delhi: Munshiram Manoharlal Publishers Pvt. Ltd.

———. 1990a. 'Problems of Understanding', *Journal of Indian Council of Philosophical Research*, Vol.VII, No.2, January–April, pp. 85–95.

Mohanty, J.N. 1992. *Reason and Tradition in Indian Thought: An Essay on the Nature of Indian Philosophical Thinking*, Oxford: Clarendon Press.

———. 2002. *The Self and its Other: Philosophical Essays*, New Delhi: Oxford University Press.

Mukherji, Nirmalangshu. 2002. 'Academic Philosophy in India', *The Economic and Political Weekly*, 9 March. pp. 931–6.

Murthy, Satchidananda, K. 1985. *Philosophy in India: Traditions, Teaching and Research*, Delhi: Motilal Banarsidass.

Nagaraj, D.R. 1993. *The Flaming Feet*, Bangalore: South Forum Press.

Namboodiripad, E.M.S. 1981. *The Mahatma and the Ism*, New Delhi: National Book Agency.

Nandy, Ashis. 1989. 'Final Encounter: The Politics of the Assassination of

Gandhi', in *At the Edge of Psychology: Essays in Politics and Culture*, New Delhi: Oxford University Press, pp. 70–98.

Nandy, Ashis. 1991. 'Hinduism and Hindutva: The Inevitability of a Confrontation', *The Times of India*, 18 February .

————. 1994. *The Illegitimacy of Nationalism: Rabindranath Tagore and the Politics of the Self*, New Delhi: Oxford University Press.

————.1995. *The Savage Freud and Other Essays on Possible and Retrievable Selves*, New Delhi: Oxford University Press.

————.1997. 'The Twilight of Certitudes: Secularism, Hindu Nationalism, and Other Masks of Deculturation', *Alternatives*, Vol. 22, No. 2, April to June, pp. 157–76.

————. 2001. *Time Warps: The Insistent Politics of Silent and Evasive Pasts*, New Delhi: Permanent Black.

Niranjana, Tejaswani. 1994. '*Roja* Revisited,' *The Economic and Political Weekly*, XXIX: 21, 21 May, p. 1299.

Odin, Steve. 1981. 'Sri Aurobindo and Hegel on the Involution-Evolution of Absolute Spirit', *Philosophy East & West*, No. 2, April, pp. 179–91.

Olson, Carl. 2002. *Indian Philosophers and Postmodern Thinkers: Dialogues on the Margins of Culture*, New Delhi: Oxford University Press.

Pantham, Thomas. 1988. 'On Modernity, Rationality and Morality: Habermas and Gandhi', *The Indian Journal of Social Sciences*, Vol. 1, No. 2, pp. 187–208.

Parekh, Bhikhu. 2000. *Rethinking Multiculturalism: Cultural Diversity and Political Theory*, New York: Palgrave.

Parel, Anthony (ed.). 1997. *M.K. Gandhi: Hind Swaraj and Other Writings*, New Delhi: Foundation Books.

Peters, Richard. 1956. *Hobbes*, Baltimore: Penguin Books.

Phillips, Stephen H. 1986. *Aurobindo's Philosophy of Brahman*, Leiden: E.J. Brill.

Pollock, Sheldon. 2002. 'Introduction: Working Papers on Sanskrit Knowledge Systems on the Eve of Colonialism', *Journal of Indian Philosophy*, Vol. 30, pp. 431–9.

Popper, Karl. 1959. *The Logic of Scientific Discovery*, London: Hutchinson.

————. 'The Development of Advaita Vedanta as a School of Philosophy', in *Radhakrishnan Centenary Volume*, eds G. Parthasarathy and D.P. Chattopadhaya, New Delhi: Oxford University Press, pp. 71–99.

Radhakrishnan, S. 1977. *Indian Philosophy*, Vol. I, London: George Allen and Unwin.

————. 2001. *An Idealist View of Life*, New Delhi: Harper Collins India.

Rajagopalachari, C. (trans.). 1976. *Mahabharata*, Chapter XX, 'The Slaying of Jarasandha', Bombay: Bharatiya Vidhya Bhavan.

Raghuramaraju, A. 1993. 'Problematising Nationalism', *The Economic and Political Weekly*, Vol. XXVIII, Nos. 27-28. 3-10 July, pp. 1433-8.

————. 1995. 'A Note on Critique and Alternative in Alasdair MacIntyre', *Journal of Indian Council of Philosophical Research*, Vol. XII, No. 2, January–April, pp. 128–36.

————. 1995a. 'Objectivism, Relativism, Pluralism: Notes on the Study of Communities and Communalism', in *Studies in Humanities and Social Sciences*, Indian Institute of Advance Study, Shimla, special issue, *Discourse and Truth*, edited by Javeed Alam, Vol. 2. Winter, pp. 217–27.

————. 1995b. 'Of Thinking Machines and Centred Self', *AI & Society*, No.9, pp. 184–92.

————. 1996. 'Gandhian Discourse in a Situated Context and a Reformulated Critique of Modernity', in *Gandhi and the Present Global Crisis*, ed. Ramashray Roy, Shimla: Indian Institute of Advanced Study, pp. 45–55.

————. 2000. 'Secularism and Time', *Social Scientist*, Vol. 28, Nos. 11–12, Nov–Dec, pp. 20–39.

————. 2005. 'West', in *The Future of Knowledge and Culture: A Dictionary for the 21st Century*, eds Vinay Lal and Ashis Nandy, Penguin, New Delhi, pp. 347-52.

Raju, P.T. 1985. *Structural Depths of Indian Thought*, Albany: State University of New York Press.

Ramanujan, A.K. 1989. 'Is there an Indian Way of Thinking?: An Informal Essay', *Contributions to Indian Sociology*, (NS) 23, pp. 41–58.

Raychaudhuri, Tapan. 1988. *Europe Reconsidered: Perceptions of the West in Nineteenth Century Bengal*. New Delhi: Oxford University Press.

————. 1999. 'Swami Vivekananda's Construction of Hinduism', in *Swami Vivekananda and the Modernisation of Hinduism*, ed. William Radice, New Delhi: Oxford University Press, pp. 264–80.

Rousseau, J.J. 1952. *The Social Contract and Discourses*, trans. with Introduction by G. D.H. Cole, London: J.M. Dent & Sons, Ltd.

Rüstau, Hiltrud. 1999. 'Swami Vivekananda's Ideal Society and Its Impact on Govind Chandra Dev', in *Swami Vivekananda and the Modernisation of Hinduism*, ed. William Radice, New Delhi: Oxford University Press, pp. 264–80.

Said, Edward. 1979. *Orientalism*, New York: Vintage Books.

————. 1984. *The World, the Text and the Critic*, London: Faber and Faber.

————. 1986. 'Orientalism Reconsidered', in *Literature, Politics and Theory: Papers from the Essex Conference 1976–84*, eds Francis Barker, Peter Hulms, et al., London: Methuen, pp. 210–29.

————. 1989. 'Representing the Colonized: Anthropology's Interlocutors', *Critical Inquiry*, Vol. 15, pp. 205–25.

————. 1994. *Culture and Imperialism*, London: Vintage.

Sarkar, Sumit. 1993. 'The Fascism of the Sangh Parivar', *Economic and Political Weekly*, 30 January, pp. 163-7.

Sartre, J.P. 2001, *Colonialism and Neocolonialism*, London: Routledge.

Savarkar, V.D. 1967. *Historical Statements*, eds S.S. Savarkar and G.M. Joshi, Bombay: Popular Prakashan.

———. 1984. 'Some of the Basic Principles and Tenets of the Hindu Movement', in *Hindu Rashtra Darshan*, 2nd edn, Bombay: Veer Savarkar Prakashan, pp. 76–90.

———. 1989. *Hindutva*, Bombay: Veer Savarkar Prakashan.

———. 2003. *Savarkar Samagra*, Vol. 7, New Delhi: Prabhat Prakashan.

Sen, A.P. 1993. *Hindu Revivalism in Bengal 1872–1905: Some Essays in Interpretation*, New Delhi: Oxford University Press.

Sen, Sanat Kumar. 1980. 'Thinking and Speaking in the Philosophy of K.C. Bhattacharyya', *Journal of Indian Philosophy*, No. 8, pp. 337–47.

Shah, K.J. 1977. 'Dissent, Protest and Reform: Some Conceptual Considerations', in *Dissent, Protest and Reform in Indian Civilization*, ed. S.C. Malik, Simla: Indian Institute of Advanced Study, pp. 70–84.

———. 1978. 'Consensus and Conflict: Some Considerations', *Indian Philosophical Quarterly*, Vol. VI, No. 1. October, pp. 101–7.

Sharma, Jyotirmaya. 2003. 'Challenging Hindutva', *Seminar*, June, pp. 31–3.

———. 2003. *Hindutva: Exploring the Idea of Hindu Nationalism*, New Delhi: Penguin Viking.

Sharma, Suresh. 1996. 'Savarkar's Quest for a Modern Hindu Consolidation.' *Studies in Humanities and Social Sciences*, Vol. II, No. 2. pp. 189–215.

Sorabji, Richard. 1996. 'The Ancient Greek Origins of the Western Debate on Animals', *Journal of Indian Council of Philosophical Research*, Vol. xii, No. 2, Jan-April, pp. 69–76.

Spivak, Gayatri Chakravorty. 1987. *In Other Worlds: Essays in Cultural Politics*, New York: Methuen.

———. 1988. 'Can the Subaltern Speak?', in *Marxism and the Interpretation of Culture*, eds Larry Grossberg and Cary Nelson, Urbana: University of Illinois Press, pp. 271–313.

———. 1993. *Outside in the Teaching Machine*, New York: Routledge.

———. 1999. *A Critique of Postcolonial Reason: Toward a History of Vanishing Present*, Cambridge: Harvard University Press.

Strauss, Leo. 1936. *Political Philosophy of Thomas Hobbes: Its Basis and Genesis*, Oxford: Oxford University Press.

———. 1964. *The City and Man*, Chicago: The University of Chicago Press.

Tagore, Rabindranath. 1985. *Nationalism*, Madras: Macmillan.

Tagore, Rabindranath. 2002. *The Religion of Man*, New Delhi: Rupa & Co.

Taylor. A. E. 1959. 'The Ethical Doctrine of Hobbes', *Philosophy*, 13, No. 52, pp. 406–24.

Taylor, Charles. 1991. *The Malaise of Modernity*. Ontario: House of Anansi Press Limited.

———. 1994. 'Justice after Virtue', in *After MacIntyre: Critical Perspective on the Work of Alasdair MacIntyre*, eds John Horton and Susan Mendus, Cambridge: Polity Press, pp. 16–43.

Tuck, Richard. 1985. *Hobbes*, Oxford: Oxford University Press.

Vivekananda, Swami. 1994. *The Complete Works of Swami Vivekananda Volumes I–VIII*, Calcutta: Advaita Ashram.

Warrender, J.H. 1957. *The Political Philosophy of Thomas Hobbes: His Theory of Obligation*, Oxford: Oxford University Press.

Watkins, J.W.M. 1965. *Hobbes' System of Ideas: Essays in the Political Significance of Philosophical Ideas*, London: Hutchinson.

Weinberger. 1975. 'Hobbes' Doctrine of Method', *American Political Science Review*, Vol. 69, pp. 1336–53.

Williams, Raymond. 1986. 'Forms of English Fiction in 1848', in *Literature, Politics and Theory: Papers from the Essex Conference 1976–84*, eds Francis Barker, Peter Hulms et al., London: Methuen, pp. 1–16.

Zaehner, R.C. 1974. *Our Savage Mind*, London: Collins.

Index

DATE DUE